RESODURCES

Sustainability is a moving target. The constant evolution in materials and processes makes keeping up with best practices a dizzying task. In the past several years designers, professional organizations, and nongovernmental organizations have created a range of great online resources that designers can take advantage of. These sites often offer the most up-to-date (and location specific) information on environmentally responsible printers, new paper products, and trends in sustainable communications design. Many also include networking, paper guides, and vendor checklists.

AIGA Center for Sustainable Design

Through case studies, interviews, resources, and discourse, this site provides information to graphic designers who want to incorporate sustainable thinking into their professional lives. www.sustainability.aiga.org

Conservatree

This site seeks to be a one-stop source for information on environmental papers. It includes information about the environmental ramifications of the paper industry and advice for both large and small-scale purchasers. www.conservatree.com

Design Can Change

This Canadian resource and networking site helps designers who want to work together to combat climate change. www.designcanchange.org

Design By Nature

This Australian site offers general information on sustainability for graphic designers including info on paper, forestry, printing, a sample print spec sheet, as well as a case studies section on the work of environmentally-conscious Australian designers. Design By Nature has some of the most extensive information on eco-friendly printing available. www.designbynature.org

SustainAble

a handbook of materials and applications for graphic designers and their clients

AARIS SHERIN

First published in the United States of America by
Rockport Publishers, a member of
Quayside Publishing Group
100 Cummings Center, Suite 406-L
Beverly, Massachusetts 01915-6101
Telephone: (978) 282-9590
Fax: (978) 283-2742
www.rockpub.com

Library of Congress Cataloging-in-Publication Data

Sherin, Aaris.

SustainAble : a handbook of materials and applications
for graphic designers and their clients / Aaris Sherin.

p. cm.

ISBN 1-59253-401-5

1. Graphic design (Typography) 2. Sustainable design. I. Title.

Z246.S45 2008

686.2'2--dc22

2007045920

ISBN-13: 978-1-59253-401-2

ISBN-10: 1-59253-401-5

10 9 8 7 6 5 4 3 2 1

Cover Design: Plan-B Studio

Layout and Design: Kathie Alexander

 Paper provided by Mohawk paper company

MOHAWK
manufactured with windpower

Printed in China

Writing this book would not have been possible without the generosity of people who share an interest in, and knowledge of, sustainable issues. Designers, paper producers, printers, activists, and business people supported and helped with the project simply because they are passionate about the topic and believed it was the right thing to do.

Laura Shore and George Milner from Mohawk, Thomas Wright and Meredith Christiansen from Neenah, Lewis Fix from Domtar, and Jeff Mendelsohn of New Leaf all provided information about sustainable paper production and many contacts. Many thanks to Holly Robbins, Wendy Brawer, Don Carli, Liza Murphy, and Jaimie Cloud, all of whom spent hours giving me a foundation with which to go forward with my research. The international representation in the book was made possible by Brenda Sanderson and the extensive rolodex at ICOGRADA. Research assistance was provided by Brian Mikesell at St. John's University, who gave me peace of mind that I hadn't overlooked the obvious. I am grateful to the designers, companies, and clients who agreed to be featured in the book; their stories continued to inspire me even when the breadth of the task seemed overwhelming.

Thanks to my editor, Emily Potts, who believed that this subject merited publication, and to my friends and family, without whom the day-to-day research and writing wouldn't have been impossible.

PRODUCING A SUSTAINABLE BOOK

When it came time to design and print this book, Rockport Publishers was eager to produce an example of sustainable design. "The best thing about this book is that it sustains itself," says production director Barbara States. She worked with Rockport's existing supply chain to specify more environmentally responsible materials, and Steve Price, founder of Plan-B Studio, took up the cause by designing the book's cover so that it reused the printing left-overs that would otherwise have been wasted.

Sustainable design means creating a communications piece that will be both innovative and visually appealing, so Price really wanted to make production part of the design. Price explains, "The production of this book (especially the cover) is about using what is 'there' already." He decided to "keep all the makeready (or color tests) from the proofing phase (some needed to be printed on a heavier stock), then simply bind the book into these. For necessary cover information, we used a demi-jacket and that was also printed on to the back side of color test sheets," says Price. The test sheets did have to go through the press a second time, but reusing this paper eliminated a great deal of the waste that would otherwise have been generated during the testing phase of the printing process.

Because Rockport prints approximately forty new graphic design titles a year, it seemed more meaningful to find ways of producing this book with eco-friendly materials using the company's existing vendors rather than going completely outside of the normal supply chain. The added benefit for Rockport's production staff was that this provided them with a wealth of information about environmentally responsible materials and processes that could be applied to the production of other titles. Rockport's printer in Asia, SNP Leefung, was willing to be flexible when it came to using specific inks and paper and reusing makeready for the job. The book was printed with vegetable-based inks on Mohawk Options eighty pound smooth 100 percent postconsumer white. "We chose to use Mohawk Options because it's beautiful paper, and Mohawk has an ongoing commitment to the environment and to working with designers by offering more sustainable choices for their projects," says Rockport editor Emily Potts.

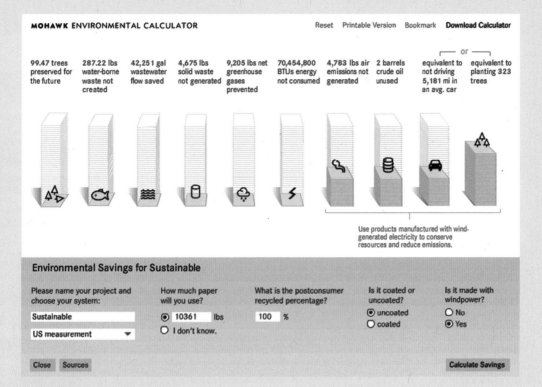

By using Mohawk's environmental calculator, it was possible to compare any additional costs incurred and environmental savings that were gained during the production of this book against other Rockport books. Hard data such as the information provided by environmental calculator as can help companies, vendors, and clients to make more informed decisions about the benefits and costs specifying environmentally preferable print production.

Mohawk uses 100 percent wind energy to power its mills, and in 2007, as part of its voluntary commitment to reduce greenhouse gas emissions, the company began to offer carbon neutral products within their production processes. "Designers used to worry about print quality when they specified recycled papers. Mohawk has worked hard to build performance into our recycled grades. Customer demand has grown rapidly as a result. It's great to see people making the right choice when they don't have to sacrifice quality and cost," says Laura Shore, senior vice president of communications at Mohawk Paper.

As the first Rockport book to be produced with environmentally friendly print production in mind, this is the most sustainable of the company's titles. "There are, of course, limits to how much we can do," notes Potts. "For example, we used the makeready sheets for the cover, but we had to use a matte laminate to protect the covers from scuffing." The reality of sustainable design is dependent on individuals making responsible choices when it comes to the materials and processes needed for the end product—whether it's a book, an annual report, or a pair of shoes.

CONTENTS

Introduction

Part One: METHODS AND THEORY

*Chapter 1: **Overview of Sustainable Design***

12 What is Sustainable Design? | **14** Corporate Sustainability: An Emerging Market
15 Paying the Bills with Socially Conscious Design | **16** How We Got Here
19 Best Practices to Design Sustainability | **20** Theoretical Framework | **24** Natural Capitalism
25 Best Practices | **25** The Problem with Green Washing

*Chapter 2: **Sustainable Motivators***

26 Why Be Socially and Environmentally Responsible?
30 Building Sustainability to Last | **36** The Next Best Chance

*Chapter 3: **The Science and Practice of Sustainable Design Forestry***

43 Forestry | **59** Paper Production | **66** Printing | **82** Recycled Paper
92 Fast Track to the Experts | **96** Waste Not, Want Not | **102** Sustainable Packaging

Part Two: PUTTING IT TO PRACTICE

*Chapter 4: **Living and Working Sustainably***

115 Viola Eco-Graphic Design | **122** Plazm Design | **126** GuerriniIsland | **134** Nau
142 Monterey Bay Aquarium | **148** Tricycle Inc. | **164** Another Limited Rebellion
170 Green Map System | **176** Two Twelve

183 *Resources*
186 *Glossary*
188 *Endnotes*
189 *Designer Index*
192 *About the Author*

*Buttons to promote eco-consciousness
designed by Hoseob Yoon, Seoul, South Korea*

INTRODUCTION

Working sustainably can be both incredibly complicated and wonderfully simple. As graphic designers we like to see ourselves as trendsetters and leaders. It therefore comes as no surprise that many designers are interested in reevaluating professional practice and improving their environmental footprint. This book is a guide to sustainable thinking and processes for the experienced professional and the inspired novice. It contains practical how-to information about production, materials, and resources as well as inspirational stories and work by leading designers. Much of the text focuses on print production, because it is the most resource intensive area in which many graphic designers work, however the book also includes sections on sustainable packaging, Web design, and environmental graphic design (EGD).

Unlike the environmental movement of the 1980s and 1990s, the sustainability movement is not motivated by guilt or doomsday thinking. It is instead led by a varied group of people who see the long-term environmental, social, and economic benefits of working sustainably. The people I interviewed included printers, mill owners, educators, and designers, and they are uniformly some of the most generous people I have ever met. Most are eager to share their experiences and are happy to refer interested parties to colleagues or friends who might have more information than they do themselves. The scores of socially and environmentally conscious designers that I talked to while researching this book were also some of the most connected and excited practitioners that I have had the pleasure of working with. This book is not an end; it is a beginning. It's an introduction to relevant theories, a survey of current production practices, and, most of all, it is an invitation to join a community.

PART ONE | # Methods and Theory

CHAPTER 1:

Overview of Sustainable Design

WHAT IS SUSTAINABLE DESIGN?

Sustainability can be defined in many ways, but perhaps the easiest way to describe it is as the balanced use of natural, social, and economic capital for the continued health of the planet and future generations. Designers can enter into the discussion and begin to adopt sustainable practices at a variety of levels depending on their individual situations. Even professionals who have spent decades immersed in this issue agree that we have yet to find the perfect ways of balancing our economic needs with the needs of the planet. Therefore, sustainable practice is more about working toward many small goals than it is about living with absolutes.

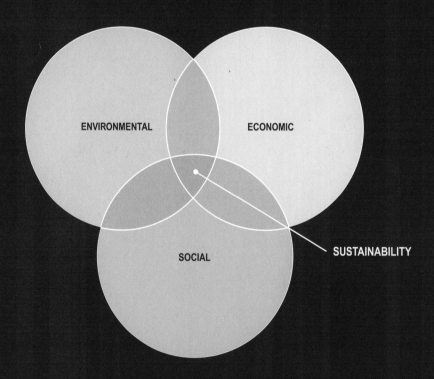

As global citizens, we have a duty to ensure that our work practices are sustainable, whatever the industry. In simple terms, it's about ensuring that the actions of today do not compromise the needs of future generations.

ANNA CARLILE – principal and founder of Viola Eco-Graphic Design

Definition of Terms

Continued debate about the legitimacy of the words "sustainable" and "sustainability" suggests that there is a need to reexamine the definitions and proper usage of these terms. In its 2002 update, the *Oxford English Dictionary* defines "sustainable" in two ways that are applicable in this text.

sus·tain·a·ble, *adjective*

1. Of, relating to, or designating forms of human economic activity and culture that do not lead to environmental degradation, esp. avoiding the long-term depletion of natural resources.

2. Utilization and development of natural resources in ways which are compatible with the maintenance of these resources, and with the conservation of the environment, for future generations.

When Brian Mikesell, associate librarian for systems and services at St. John's University (Queens, New York), was asked whether sustainability is in fact a "real" word, he responded, "of course it is." He explains, "The contemporary use of the term in relation to the environment is merely a shorthand reference and could easily be expressed more lengthily by something like sustainable development or sustainable agriculture or environmentally sustainable tourism etc., thus the term in its new usage becomes a derivative of the original, and its full meaning can only be determined by context."

"Eco-friendly," "green," "eco-design," and similar expressions are frequently used to refer to processes and concepts that value environmental responsibility. Some designers and experts prefer to use these terms in addition to or instead of "sustainable." While not necessarily incorrect, it is important to understand that terms such as "green" and "eco-friendly" primarily refer to the environment, whereas "sustainability" also considers the social and economic implications of materials, designs, and production processes.

CORPORATE SUSTAINABILITY:
AN EMERGING MARKET

Practicing sustainable design isn't just about doing the right thing; it's also a way of taking advantage of an emerging market. Hank Stewart of Green Team Advertising in New York has seen an increase in the number of brands that want to make social and environmental ideals part of their core brand values. "Consumers are awakening to the power they wield in the marketplace, and companies are afraid that they are losing out because their competition stands for something that they don't." In recent years, Nike, Chiquita, and BP have all chosen to use environmentally preferable production practices for their annual reports, and many Fortune 500 companies also produce corporate sustainability reports or corporate citizenship reports (CSR) in addition to traditional annual reports. CSRs highlight the environmental and social commitment of a company and almost always require some degree of sustainable production. Derek Smith, a consultant on paper and the environment says, "Many large organizations today have strong environmental philosophies, but too frequently those philosophies don't end up in the companies' practices."

PAYING THE BILLS WITH
SOCIALLY CONSCIOUS DESIGN

There is little point in making a hard distinction between socially and environmentally conscious design because sustainability requires the melding of the two. However, there is an emerging specialization in design for social causes and nonprofits. Though definitely still a niche market, this area of practice is growing, and today studios that have chosen to limit their client base are thriving. Design Action Collective in Oakland, California, balances their efforts to reduce their environmental footprint with a desire to work with clients and vendors that share their values. Innosanto Nagara, founding member of Design Action Collective, explains, "Most of our clients are actively working for a sustainable world. There is little point in saving a few trees by using recycled paper if the client you are working for is destroying the environment or harming the community." He notes that even if a designer is working for a nonprofit company, it is vital to consider both the social and environmental record of the vendors that one chooses. He says, "We are a certified green business, a worker-owned cooperative, and a union shop; amongst our vendors we give strong preference to those who are similarly organized." Mixing values and creative passion is a powerful combination, and many graphic designers find that they can work with like-minded organizations, support social causes, and still pay the bills.

Innosanto Nagara says, "Amazon Watch annual reports need to really take their supporters and funders in North America to the Amazon. We do show images of destruction in the reports, but the covers focus on a positive view of what is at stake. The reports were printed at 8.5" x 8.5" because it was the most efficient size for the green printer we use to get the most out of a sheet. They were printed on 100 percent postconsumer recycled paper with soy inks at Inkworks, which is a union shop."

HOW WE GOT HERE

It is widely agreed that *Silent Spring*, Rachel Carson's 1962 book connecting human impact to the environment, was a catalyst for the modern day environmental movement. However, the ideas of two lesser-known visionaries, Buckminster Fuller and Victor Papanek, began inspiring designers to consider their roles in environmental degradation and social inequity long before it was cool to be green.

Buckminster Fuller

Buckminster Fuller's work can be seen as a forerunner to the contemporary sustainability movement. An inventor, scientist, writer, and environmental activist, Fuller believed in doing more with less. He was concerned about humanity's wasteful use of resources and observed that, "Men have felt that they could dispose of annoyingly accruing substances with which they did not know how to deal by dispatching them outward in some cosmic direction, assumedly to be defused innocuously and infinitely." He thought that humans acquire technology for the wrong reasons and was a proponent of social equity and even dispersal of wealth among the world's population. Believing that more positive alternatives were possible he wrote, "Humanity could acquire technology for the purpose of total success and enduring peace for humanity." During his life, Fuller was often ridiculed as a utopian whose work had little practical application, and few of his inventions were ever produced. Nevertheless, Fuller's ideas about the integration of natural systems and human invention and his advocacy for environmental issues have been inspirational to many designers, environmentalists, and scholars who advocate the responsible use of the planet's remaining resources.

Fuller began designing his most famous invention, the geodesic dome, in the 1950s and was awarded a patent for his invention in 1954. This image is of the geodesic dome of the American pavilion at the Montreal Expo 1967.

Our planet Earth is home to all humans, but scientifically speaking it belongs only to the universe. It belongs equally to all humans. This is the natural, geometrical law. Any laws of men which contradict nature are unenforceable and specious.

— BUCKMINSTER FULLER

Victor Papanek

Originally trained as an industrial designer, Victor Papanek challenged designers of all kinds to take responsibility for the social and environmental ramifications of their work. Beginning in the 1970s with his publication *Design for the Real World* (Academy Chicago Publishers, 1972), Papanek suggested a renewed focus on the end user and believed that designers had an obligation to work for the greater good and not just the financial well-being of their clients. He railed against built-in obsolescence saying that, "In all pollution, designers are implicated at least partially." The definition of a designer put forth by Papanek is that of a fully thinking problem solver. It is a role both more powerful than that of visual stylist and one that requires greater accountability. In his second book, *The Green Imperative* (Thames and Hudson, 1995), Papanek included "the wisdom to anticipate the environmental, ecological, economic, and political consequences of design intervention" in his list of the skills and talents that a designer should possess. He went on to question "whether designers, architects, and engineers can be held personally responsible and legally liable for creating tools, objects, appliances, and buildings that bring about environmental deterioration." Papanek was ahead of his time. When *Design for the Real World* was first published, he was denounced by colleagues and asked to resign from his professional association. By the mid-1990s when his second book, *The Green Imperative*, was published, public opinion had evolved, and many of Papanek's ideas have been adopted by contemporaries who had originally been skeptical.

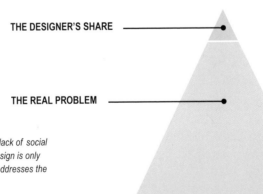

THE DESIGNER'S SHARE

THE REAL PROBLEM

Papanek created this diagram to explain the lack of social engagement in design. He suggested that design is only concerned with a very small role and rarely addresses the real needs.

-From *Designing for the Real World*

by Eric Benson, assistant professor of
graphic design at the University of Illinois
and founder of re-nourish.com

BEST PRACTICES TO DESIGN SUSTAINABLY

Creating sustainable pieces should begin at the start of the design process. First, the designer must determine if the project deserves to exist in a tangible form. To do this, the designer should ask the following questions:

- Is this the best method to communicate the message?
- What is the impact of making this piece?
- How can we lessen the impact if we print the piece?

After this initial discussion, it is important to openly communicate ideas and decisions with the design team and client. It is imperative for the graphic designer to be educated about sustainability and to discuss project goals at length before embarking on any design endeavor. Educating oneself is just as important as educating one's client. As the project continues to develop, the graphic designer should work collaboratively with the client and vendors to create a solution that follows these five sustainable principles:

- Respect and care for the community.
- Improve the quality of life.
- Conserve Earth's vitality and diversity.
- Minimize the depletion of nonrenewable resources.
- Change personal attitudes and practices to keep with the planet's carrying capacity.

Each of these principles, in turn, encourage the designer to make the following, more conscious, design decisions:

- Design for re-use/longevity.
- Design cyclically, not linearly.
- Choose recycled/nontoxic materials.
- Minimize waste (e.g., use entire press sheet).
- Minimize ink coverage.
- Choose local vendors that use renewable energy and employ socially equitable and environmentally friendly business practices.
- Educate consumers about the lifecycle issues through messaging/marketing.
- Encourage others to design sustainably.

Because designers are both makers and consumers, our power to incite change is compelling. If we help to change the way our world is designed, it will allow for a better quality of life and a continuing viable economic future.

THEORETICAL FRAMEWORK

Sustainability, like good design, relies on conceptual and theoretical frameworks as well as technical competencies. Just as we wouldn't consider our software skills to be a good indicator of design ability, eco-friendly printing is largely ineffectual if one doesn't understand the thinking that makes it necessary. Graphic designers are at an advantage when it comes to adopting sustainable practices. We are accustomed to conceptual problem solving and systems thinking. For most designers, taking on sustainability will require a subtle shift in thinking and practice but not the rejection of previously held beliefs.

Biomimicry

In her 1997 book, *Biomimicry: Innovation Inspired by Nature*, author Janine Benyus suggests that because nature has spent the past 3.8 billion years engineering systems and processes that work symbiotically in their environments, it should be the standard from which to assess the "rightness of our innovations." Biomimicry (from "bios," meaning life, and "mimesis," meaning to imitate) imitates or takes inspiration from natural models to create designs that solve human problems.[1] Increasingly natural systems are being disturbed and irrevocably altered by human activity. Nature-inspired designs offer some of the most hopeful solutions for ways and products that can help us live more sustainably. In the past, our inability to understand many aspects of biology and interconnected systems may have been excuses not to follow nature's lead. However, developments in observation techniques and understanding of biology at cellular and subcellular levels have allowed us greater access to the science of the natural world than ever before. Researchers, designers, engineers, architects, and even economists are studying how organisms and ecosystems work and applying that thinking to useful products and services. Nature-inspired designs are already being used with varied applications including packaging, adhesion systems, transportation, and energy production.

Principles of Biomimicry	Nature runs on sunlight. Nature uses only the energy it needs. Nature fits form to function. Nature recycles everything. Nature rewards cooperation. Nature banks on diversity. Nature demands local expertise. Nature curbs excesses from within. Nature taps the power of limits.[2]

Questions to ask of innovations inspired by nature:	1. Will it fit in? 2. Will it last? 3. Is there a precedent for this nature? If the preceding questions were answered in the affirmative, then the innovation or product design should also adhere to the principles of biomimicry.[3]

Here's an example of biomimicry that you have heard of: In 1948, after a walk in the Alps left him covered with thistle spurs, Swiss-born electrical engineer George de Mestral was inspired to develop a useful product. De Mestral examined the annoying barbs under a microscope and saw that tiny plant hooks were able to take hold of fabric and animal fur. Patented in 1955, Velcro (with hook and loop fasteners) is now a multimillion dollar business and an efficient way to fasten fabrics and other materials.

Biomimicry is the conscious emulation of life's genius and innovation inspired by nature.

JANINE BENYUS – author of *Biomimicry*

Cradle to Cradle

In their seminal 2002 text, *Cradle to Cradle* (North Point Press), William McDonaugh and Michael Braungart proposed that products should be designed so that after their useful lives are over they can provide "nourishment" for something new. McDonaugh and Braungart don't categorically denounce commerce or industry. Instead, they see flawed design models rather than consumption as the most pressing problem. McDonaugh and Braungart advocate more intelligent and ecological design as a solution for sustainable prosperity.

Cradle to cradle principles are guided by the notion that in the natural world waste equals food and that there is no reason for human activity to be inherently wasteful and destructive. McDonaugh and Braungart argue that using the term "recycling" to describe the current system of recovery and reuse is somewhat disingenuous. They suggest that the contemporary industrial model is essentially a cradle to grave approach. We "downcycle" rather that recycle. With each subsequent use we produce lower grade material until we are finally left with unusable waste that can only be incinerated or stored in landfills. "Unless materials are specifically designed to ultimately become safe food for nature, composting can present problems as well. When so-called biodegradable municipal wastes, including packaging and paper, are composted, the chemicals and toxins in the materials can be released into the environment," according to McDonaugh and Braungart. Instead of focusing on the difficult task of reusing (or recycling) materials not initially designed for a second and third life, McDonaugh and Braungart suggest that we are in need of an industrial re-evolution in which we will eliminate the concept of waste and instead design products and systems that can provide nourishment for something new at the end of their useful lives.

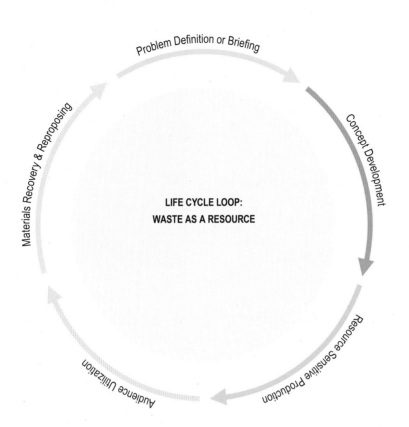

Problem Definition or Briefing

Concept Development

Resource Sensitive Production

Audience Utilization

Materials Recovery & Reproposing

LIFE CYCLE LOOP:
WASTE AS A RESOURCE

Cradle to Cradle in Use	Using cradle to cradle principles, people and industries could produce the following: • Buildings that, similar to trees, produce more energy than they consume and purify their own waste water • Factories that produce effluents that are drinking water • Products that, when their useful lives are over, do not become useless waste but can be tossed onto the ground to decompose and become food for plants and animals and nutrients for the soil or that can return to industrial cycles to supply high-quality raw materials for new products • Billions, even trillions, of dollars worth of materials accrued for human and natural purposes each year • Transportation that improves the quality of life while delivering goods and services • A world of abundance, not one of limits, pollution, and waste[4]

NATURAL CAPITALISM

There are economists, environmentalists, and scientists who argue that respecting the environment and being socially responsible can actually increase a company's profitability. *Natural Capitalism* (Little Brown and Company, 1999) by Paul Hawken, Amory Lovings, and Hunter Lovings is full of tangible examples of how businesses can thrive by achieving a balance between life and commerce. *Natural Capitalism* introduces the idea that we are entering a new phase of industrialism, characterized by the loss of living systems, emerging scarcity, and the need to begin valuing natural capital. The authors suggest that appreciating living systems for their tangible worth will require a reevaluation of traditional assumptions about capitalism. To enable people, governments, and businesses to value all capital, including natural capital, Hawken and the Lovings suggest the implementation of four strategies.

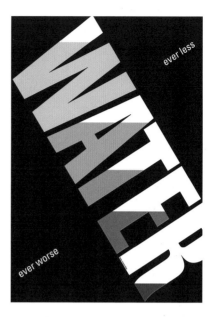

Poster for "Water, ever less, ever worse," designed for the water collection of *Bibliotheca Alexandrina*, 2007. Designer Armando Milani says, "Designers have a sociopolitical task, which goes beyond merely making something attractive and saleable. Messages must be sharp, strong, and memorizable."

1. **Radical resource productivity** slows resource depletion, lowers pollution, and provides a basis to increase worldwide employment with meaningful jobs.

2. **Biomimicry** reduces wasteful output of materials; can be accomplished by redesigning industrial or biological lines.

3. **Service and flow economy** is based on the flow of economic services that can better protect the ecosystem services upon which it depends.

4. **Investing in natural capital** works to reverse worldwide planetary destruction through reinvestments in sustaining, restoring, and expanding stocks of natural capital.[5]

We screw up sometimes, but we own up to our mistakes and keep moving forward, questioning assumptions in our effort to get better. Question us. Challenge everything we do ... It's the only way we can really improve.

— Nau Statement of Purpose, www.nau.com

BEST PRACTICES

"Best practices" is a phrase that appears often in this book, yet it is not a concrete term that can be used to describe a specific set of standards or objectives. Instead, it is a pragmatic way of referring to production and business practices that attempt to choose the best environmental and social options for the moment. Technology, processes, and materials constantly evolve so what is considered best practices today may be merely passé in five years or even six months. This publication does not attempt to quantify a perfect set of standards, instead we encourage designers to investigate a range of materials and processes and adopt those that most closely fit their level of commitment and the production requirements.

THE PROBLEM WITH GREEN WASHING

As more consumers begin to make purchases based at least partially on a company's values, it can be tempting for businesses to hype their commitment to environmental or social causes simply in the hopes of bettering their bottom line. Green washing is a concern for both the savvy consumer and committed activists, with the latter worried that consumers who feel burned by green companies may turn their backs on an evolving industry. As early as 1995, Jon Entine wrote an article for the *Utne Reader* titled "Green Washing" in which he expressed concern that the dramatic increase in "cause-related marketing might lead to green practices being replaced by green washing." Entine suggests that transparency, openness, and honesty are the ways to combat green washing and are the qualities that customers should look for from the brands, products, and services that they use. Entine's advice from more than a decade ago still holds true today. The best weapon against green washing is informed purchasing, coupled with knowledge and curiosity. Look for companies that report their activities transparently in every sector of their businesses and have plans for how they will increase their social and environmental initiatives in the future.

CHAPTER 2:

Sustainable Motivators

People become more environmentally and socially conscious for many reasons, and concern for the environment isn't at the top of everyone's list. Some people have ethical concerns about employees' work conditions, others wish to avoid risk, and many worry about the state of the world that their children will live in. Once one understands what motivates companies and individuals to be interested in sustainability it becomes easier to talk about the topic with clients, supervisors, and coworkers. Sonora Beam, principal of Digital Hive EcoLogical Design, suggests that sustainability is about pragmatism as well as idealism. "Negative or punishing messages aren't a real motivator for behavior change," she says. Beam advises designers, "not to let the perfect get in the way of the good." This section includes a list of proven motivators, practical advice on how to talk with clients, an examination of what it takes to become a sustainable design studio, and a brief look at issues of sustainability in education.

WHY BE SOCIALLY AND ENVIRONMENTALLY RESPONSIBLE?

Jaimie Cloud, founder of the Cloud Institute for Sustainability Education, is an expert on what motivates people to become more socially and environmentally responsible. She maintains that most people want to do the right thing and reframes common questions to help her audience understand the importance of sustainable thinking. To the designer who loves the tactile feel of the perfect sheet of paper she asks, "Would you choose beauty over life when you can have both? Do you stand for perfect paper texture today over the ability to get paper in ten years?" Cloud believes that we live in a world linked together by mutually beneficial systems and that every action should solve more than one problem.

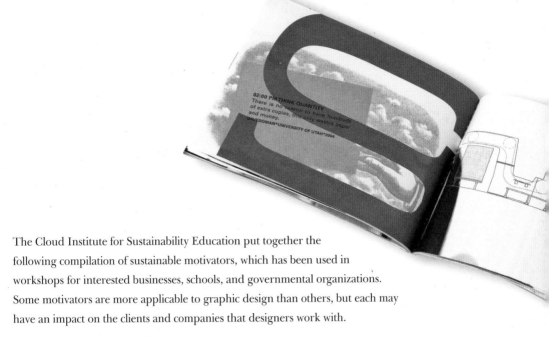

The Cloud Institute for Sustainability Education put together the following compilation of sustainable motivators, which has been used in workshops for interested businesses, schools, and governmental organizations. Some motivators are more applicable to graphic design than others, but each may have an impact on the clients and companies that designers work with.

Managing Reputation and Brand Value

Reputation has real financial value in today's market. People often purchase a company's products and services because they trust the company and believe the company is a force for good in the world. The company's brand is associated with positive ideas, values, and feelings in the mind of the consumer. If such a company is revealed to be dishonest, unfair to its workers, or destructive to the planet, the consumer will be less likely to purchase the goods or the services of that company. Respected companies also attract quality employees.

Protecting the Right to Operate

Companies that are socially and environmentally responsible earn the public's trust. That trust is financially valuable because the company doesn't have to spend time and money answering to regulators and proving that they are complying with laws, and they avoid costly fines and lawsuits.

Reduce Waste *summarizes some of the things that Carol Sogard and her students at the University of Utah learned about environmentally friendly print and design. With reuse in mind, the piece is produced by reprinting on top of unused posters with an offset press.*

Developing an Ongoing Relationship with Customers

Business practices that preserve resources also keep a company's product in the hands of their customers longer and create long-term needs for services. For example, Interface Carpet doesn't just sell customers carpet; they provide carpet maintenance for years and replace worn squares as needed. Xerox doesn't sell its customers "throwaway" copy machines, but rather establishes long-term leases with them. The company saves money by recycling, and it makes a steady income from maintaining its customers' copiers. Rather than a one-time deal, you can bank on a steady, long-term source of revenue.

It Pays

Often, being socially and environmentally responsible has financial benefits. Recycling and reusing material saves money and generates income. Treating employees well results in increased productivity and less turnover, so you don't have to spend money training a new workforce. Socially and ecologically responsible companies consistently outperform other companies in most industries, which means more profits and higher stock prices for those companies.

Be Pioneers in New Markets

Consumers around the world are increasingly seeing the impact of their consumption decisions on their environment and their own health. Conscious consumption—from fuel-efficient cars to organic foods—is a rapidly growing market. Consumers also realize their purchasing power and are pressuring companies to be more responsible and sustainable. These demands have meant not only new corporate design and production but also new regulations for eco-friendly and socially responsible corporate behavior. You can be ready for the growth in demand for socially responsible businesses, and you can be first to grab customer loyalty and brand recognition by offering environmentally sustainable products and services now.

Be Able to Attract Employees Who Can Thrive in the Twenty-First Century

More and more people, young and not so young, are looking to integrate their work lives with their values, their ethics, and their knowledge of interdependent systems. "The best and brightest" want to work for companies they can be proud to represent and companies that help them live healthy, productive, whole lives.

SustainAbility (www.sustainability.com); Innovest (www.innovestgroup.com); KPMG, "The Business Case for Sustainability;" World Resources Institute, "The Next Bottom Line"

When the information-services, news, and media company Bloomberg decided to replace their stationery and collateral with a new look, the company's design team recognized an opportunity to create an example of sustainable design. Their mission to evolve old business cards into functional and beautiful objects that would be enjoyed by employees worldwide brought them to MIO, a design firm recognized for working with materials that advance sustainable goals.

The end result of MIO and Bloomberg's collaboration was a stool. Each seat has a tag that states, "This chair was created with recycled Bloomberg business cards, contributed by employees all over the world."

by Cheryl Heller, CEO
Heller Communication Design

BUILDING SUSTAINABILITY TO LAST

When I first became interested in sustainability and systems thinking several years ago, all the examples I read about had to do with manufacturing or sourcing, or use of energy and natural resources. I couldn't find anyone who had applied the principles of sustainability to what I do. Simply put, I help companies figure out who they are, what they stand for, and how to use communications to engage their stakeholders in helping to make it real.

I made two assumptions. First, if we are to live sustainably, then we must apply these principles to everything we do, and second, anything we do must be susceptible to improvement through the application of these principles. So I spent a great deal of time trying to figure out how to apply these principles to my work. Systems thinking teaches that there are no independent events; everything is connected. It also teaches that in order to solve problems, you have to start upstream where things are initiated, rather than downstream where they are executed.

It's fairly simple to see communications as a connected system, both within the company from which it originates and in the world outside. And it's impossible not to see the waste inherent in this system—including useless meetings, too many people involved in the simplest things and too few people involved in other things to make them successful, office politics, competition where there should be collaboration, wasted efforts, wasted energy, and wasted materials. And above all, a scary comfort level with hyperbole and generalities, a sameness to so many of the things created, and a laziness in seeking and telling the truth.

To make a very long story short, I came to a couple of conclusions, described in the paragraphs that follow, that have changed what I do and how I do it dramatically. In general, the only way to make communications sustainable is to align messages with behavior. It saves an enormous amount of effort and money, plus all that time spent making things up if you simply do what you say and say what you do. Second, the only way to impact communications in a lasting way is to start upstream; with the CEO, and with the brand.

We do a great deal of work now for nongovernmental organizations, including World Wildlife Fund, Audubon, Wildlife Trust, International Development Enterprises, and SafeHorizon, the leading crisis assistance organization for battered children and spouses. We look for ways to connect what they do with the needs of our corporate clients.

CREATIVE DIRECTION: **CHERYL HELLER**, ART DIRECTION: **SARAH BERENDS**
DESIGN: **DEVON BERGER**, PHOTO: GALAPAGOS: **STEVEN MORELLO**
PHOTO: **FRANS LANTING**, WWFCOVER: **STEVE BLOOM**

If you have trouble talking to clients about making their brands sustainable, just think about the alternative. Imagine a future in which you don't bring the subject up. It might go like this:

You go on making things, and thinking of ways of talking your clients into making more things because that's what you like to do. Keep your head a foot or so from your monitor and stay focused on finding the perfect font for that capabilities brochure. You find your services abandoned because your client is a lot smarter than you and sees the big picture. You find that you were the only one not talking to him or her about it.

The Future of the World Really Does Depend on Our Ability to Communicate with and Understand Each Other

What if those of us who are skilled at communicating could really make a difference? How can we get people's attention and begin to tell the truth? How can we learn to listen differently so that we know what the truth is? We need to think about communication differently now. For starters, we have to come to grips with what's at stake: the planet, animals, and everybody we know and love. Genuinely accepting this changes things. It puts all that we do in a different context, and makes every opportunity we have to connect with people—and move them—a little more precious, and a lot harder to squander on inanities. Sometimes it makes it hard to talk about anything else.

In the Future, Corporations Will Be More Responsible in Their Roles as Citizens

Today, information of all kinds is easier to come by, and people are paying attention. Some companies are embracing the opportunity and leading the way to real triple bottom lines (see glossary page 186). Others are in various stages of migration to it. But rarely will you find a company disinterested in having a conversation about how to become a better corporate citizen. This goes beyond using recycled paper, although that's an important thing to do. It's beyond having a foundation that supports the local opera, although we're grateful for that, too. It means companies being responsible for the harm they cause the planet and for the way they treat people, as well as the profit they make. It is now called corporate citizenship, and it includes what people typically think of as sustainability.

The Sappi Ideas That Matter *program and identity. This was the first program I developed that engaged a client in corporate citizenship and corporate responsibility. It's about eight years old now and still going.*

CREATIVE DIRECTION: **CHERYL HELLER,**
DESIGNER: **VERONICA OH**

It's important to remember that communication should be fun, and humor is almost always a great way to win people over.

CREATIVE DIRECTION: **CHERYL HELLER**
ART DIRECTION: **SARAH BERENDS**
DESIGNER: **DEVON BERGER**
PHOTO: **STEPHEN GREEN-ARMYTAGE**

All of the work we do starts with an investigation of systems.

CHERYL HELLER – CEO, Heller Communication Design

This Trend Will Continue, and Those Companies Left Behind Will Indeed be Left Behind

What that means for most of us who work for corporations is that we have a lot of learning to do to get up to speed. We have to know as much as our clients do about what corporate citizenship is about. And we have to understand the role that communication plays in it, and how we can help them become better citizens. If we don't, we will be left out of the conversation as well.

Everybody Already Knows It

I have found that having the conversation with clients is a relief—for them and for me. It's exactly the same feeling you get when you tell somebody the truth about something you were worried about, and they get it. Corporations can begin to frame their citizenship around the things they are proud of, and just as successfully, they can create new initiatives around those things about their companies that make them feel most vulnerable. Or, they can take on the very simple things that they could accomplish as an organization if they just made the effort.

Read your clients' mission statements, if you haven't already. Every company has one, and quite a few of them already include some form of social responsibility. Those that don't refer to corporate responsibility explicitly can be reinterpreted to include it. Even if a company's mission statement includes "making quality products" or giving customers the "best price," it's a good place to start.

Help your clients redefine quality so that it includes quality of life for everyone, including all living things on the planet. That would make them think about sourcing, processes, waste, etc. Or, help them rethink "best price" as the real price of goods, instead of the list price, as Lester Brown defines in his extraordinary book, *Plan B 2.0.* For example, the real cost of a box of strawberries shipped to Boston from California includes the cost to the environment of the CO^2 emissions from transport, the cost of the fossil fuels used to keep them refrigerated, the cost of health care for increased childhood asthma due to poor air quality, etc. Brown believes that only by recognizing the real price we're paying for all goods will we get the attention needed to create real change.

Any consideration of sustainability should begin with nature. This is the cover of a promotional brochure for Sappi Paper—a faux annual report for a zoo, written by the inmates.

CREATIVE DIRECTION: CHERYL HELLER
PHOTO: ELLIOT SCHWARTZ
WRITER: PETER CAROLINE

Behavior Is the Most Powerful Form of Communication

Talking to a CEO about what his or her company stands for is exciting. The result is a definition of the company's compelling purpose, and when a purpose is compelling, it's because it shoots a good deal higher and is far more engaging than the next quarter's earnings. Start the conversation by asking, "How do we have to behave, as a company, in order to make the mission statement a reality?" The process is an iterative one, and it entails looking at everything the company does and asking how it can evolve to be more in line with the promise of the mission.

Often, much can be accomplished by simply informing customers about where materials for a product come from, or how they can recycle it after they're finished using it. Many companies are afraid of transparency because they think they'll become the target of activist groups, but customers and employees will know honest effort and intent when they see it.

Hopefully, this will lead your clients to much more in-depth conversations of their own about other aspects of the companies' business that are outside your purview.

Finding the Words

If you've seen the documentary *The Corporation*, you know that after the Civil War, some wily corporate lawyers won the same rights for corporations that were intended for newly freed slaves. These lawyers found a way to classify corporations as individuals, and it opened the door for them to pursue their "inalienable rights" with far less restriction than might otherwise have been granted. The problem is, of course, that the laws that govern individuals' behavior do not govern corporations, so there is no system of checks and balances. Corporations are free to go after each other and fight to the death, and they are rewarded for it rather than punished. A corporation isn't born with a sense of ethics and responsibility that guides its actions. It has to create its own value system and instill it in all its employees through constant communication.

Nobody says less than the Finns, and they pride themselves on being the most honest people in the world. (They even have research to prove it.) They do indeed set an example for us all, in terms of sustainability.

CLIENT: **STORA ENSO**
CREATIVE DIRECTOR: **CHERYL HELLER**
PHOTO EDITOR: **ALICE ROSE GEORGE**

Today we are witnessing a society that increasingly expects corporations to have ethics, and also to declare them.

Putting what a company stands for into words that are not clichéd is a difficult thing to do, but it's worth any effort to accomplish. One of the greatest challenges that companies face is how to find a distinctive and honest voice for their communications.

Communication Is a Tool for Engagement

Once the words have been found that define what your clients stand for, the next step is to get people excited about helping to make it true, beginning with everyone who works in the company. The basic elements of communication are what you'll need to call upon: a clear idea of what you want to say, what it might mean to the people who hear it, and what you would like them to do about it.

Internal communications tend to be static and one-way, often sent out as "news" from management, without an invitation to respond. Creating ways for employees to participate is the only way to earn their attention.

Having the Courage to Say Less

One of the things that we, as people who make things, need to think about is whether the thing we're being hired to make is actually worth it. Or if it could be done more simply, or if the three things that kind of sort of work could be done better as one. Its goes against every instinct instilled in us to shrink our assignments instead of growing them, but just as companies need to think about the waste they produce, and find new opportunities through sustainable practices, so do we. And by the way, hidden in the sentence above is the secret to where your new work will come from. This is the opportunity to evolve from being paid for how much you do to being paid for how well you think.

THE NEXT BEST CHANCE

Whether it is new software or cutting-edge typographic styles, educators are expected to be at the forefront of their disciplines. They are in a key position to expose students to new competencies and theoretical shifts. Once sparked, an awareness of sustainable issues cannot be unlearned. One can no longer help evaluating book design, packaging, and brochures not only for evidence of creative skill, but also for environmentally responsible production and the visual marks that indicate third party certifications or use of recycled content. Many professionals believe that incorporating sustainable thinking into educational programs will lead to its widespread adoption in professional practice.

Kelly Salchow, assistant professor of graphic design at Michigan State University, says, "By solving recurring problems in alternative ways, we can improve our surroundings not only visually and functionally, but also environmentally." Salchow incorporates concepts on sustainable thinking and environmental responsibility into classes that range from User Experience to Design Process and Concepts. "My students recognize that graphic design has the power to improve or detract from many facets of our environment, and they welcome the challenge to justify and understand the entire lifecycle of what they design."

The theme for the 2003 AIGA Design Conference, "Power of Design," focused on sustainable design issues. The conference website stated, "Designers will play critical roles in the success of our rebounding economy, both as agents of social change in a complex world and as leading architects of sustainable solutions for a troubled planet." Many participants left the conference inspired to reevaluate the ramifications of their creative output. Attendee Carol Sogard, an associate professor at the University of Utah, first thought that she would simply tweak projects and develop a new syllabus for one class, however, as she learned more she also began to reassess her own practice. With funding from her university, Sogard enrolled in the Sustainable Design Online certificate program offered at Minneapolis College of Art and Design (MCAD) and has worked with her local AIGA chapter to reach out to her community through an event called "Live Green: Eco Exchange Downtown."

Short group project by Carol Sogard's undergraduate students at the University of Utah. Students were given two hours to invent a company that had a green initiative as its primary goal. The company name, logo, and a poster needed to be developed within the allocated time.

FESPOD: FRIENDS OF ENEMIES OF STRESS, POLLUTION AND OIL DEPENDENCY WAS DESIGNED BY ZAK JENSEN, ANDY SORTOR, AND MIDORI WATANUKI.

GREEN SPACE: AN OPEN SPACE PLANNING INITIATIVE WAS DESIGNED BY MATT TAYLOR, AAAEN ESPLIN, VANESSA HOLZ, AND DONALD THOMSON.

I get eleven miles to the banana.

By not driving your car, you can save money, reduce oil dependency, avoid air pollution, and contribute to your physical and mental health.

FESPOD
Friends of Enemies of Stress, Pollution and Oil Dependency

space
because living next to midvale sucks.

green space

Educating Professionals

Sustainable Design Online may be the best way for designers to learn about sustainability in a guided setting. The MCAD certificate program was created for working professionals to improve their knowledge of sustainable practice, theory, and techniques. Students can enroll in a single course or take the full eighteen credit certificate program. Classes range from general courses such as Elements of Sustainability: A Foundation and Innovation, Sustainability and Design to discipline specific classes like Packaging Design and Market Greening Design: Green-Eco Design and Green Marketing. Because the program is on-line, MCAD is able to draw faculty with extensive expertise in the field, including Dayna Baumeister, cofounder of the Biomimicry Guild.

The options for people who want environmental and social consciousness incorporated into their educational programs are growing, with many schools adding one or more classes related to sustainability in existing curricula. A number of MBA programs now include an environmental track, and though this may be a good option for some, graphic designers are probably better served by programs that are tailored to meet the specific production and theoretical needs of design disciplines.

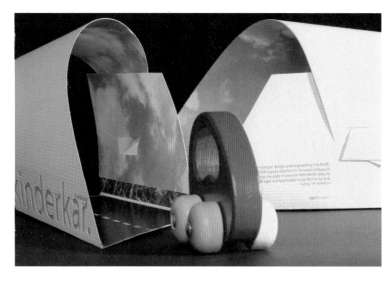

Student Kim Magerko's packaging for Kinderkar created from paper without the use of adhesives

Class Projects

Because of the complexity of materials often required, package design projects can provide the ideal subject matter for students to explore sustainable thinking. At the University of Illinois Urbana Champaign, Eric Benson has his Advanced Graphic Design 1 class tackle the design of packaging for a new line of tea using principles from William McDonough and Michael Braungart's *Cradle to Cradle*.

Students were asked to target their solutions to an audience of highly-educated, savvy tea consumers and differentiate Mode Tea's packaging from its competitors. Designs had to be cost effective and reflect the company's commitment to the environment by using eco-friendly materials. Undergraduate bachelor's of fine arts degree student Austin Happel came up with a design that was lightweight and used compostable Polylactide (PLA) bioplastics. "The package itself is designed to weigh a minimal amount and becomes stackable during shipping (cutting freight charges) and on the shelf. The package doesn't need any shrink wrapping due to its sturdy construction from PLA, a corn-based plastic, and because vegetable-based ink was used the entire package could be composted," says Benson.

Austin Happel's design for Mode Tea. Materials: PLA (polyactic acid), corn-based plastic, vegetable ink.

Kelly Salchow's undergraduate Design Process and Concepts class at Michigan State University used paper constructions to create sustainable packaging. Salchow gave each student this brief.

Reusable packaging brief: Each student began with a generic toy and experimented loosely with three-dimensional constructions in paper. The package was required to have durable value, functioning at first as a protective layer for the product, and later being integrated into the experience of use. The continued function of the package elongates its lifecycle, although it is ultimately biodegradable.

Student Kim Magerko created a design solution titled Kinderkar. The exterior of the package clearly displayed the toy with a diecut, held in place with tension. When Kinderkar is removed, the diecut is reversed, creating a tunnel of roadway and open air. The package becomes part of the landscape for Kinderkar to travel in, integrating a secondary function and prolonging its use.

CHAPTER 3:

The Science and Practice of Sustainable Design

Paper production is the fourth most energy-intensive of all manufacturing industries. It is also one of the dirtiest, generating air and water pollution as well as solid waste.[1] Today, paper makes up more than 30 percent of the waste in municipal landfills, and 75 percent of the communications pieces we design end up in the trash within a year. Even with the rapid growth in e-commerce and digital delivery systems, paper consumption has not decreased. The U.S. per capita consumption of paper products is the highest in the world—approximately 750 pounds per year—with Europe and Japan running close behind.

Adding to the problem globally, the appetite for paper products continues to grow in low and middle-income countries that have historically used far less paper than the developed world. At every point in the lifecycle of this essentially disposable material there are options for reducing its impact on the environment and social systems. Specifying environmentally preferable paper products and working with eco-friendly printers can greatly reduce the effect that graphic design has on the planet.

In the case of larger companies and integrated mills, many of the following steps may come under the umbrella of one company. However, in some cases there can be up to ten different companies involved in the supply chain of print production.

LINKS IN THE SUPPLY CHAIN OF PAPER

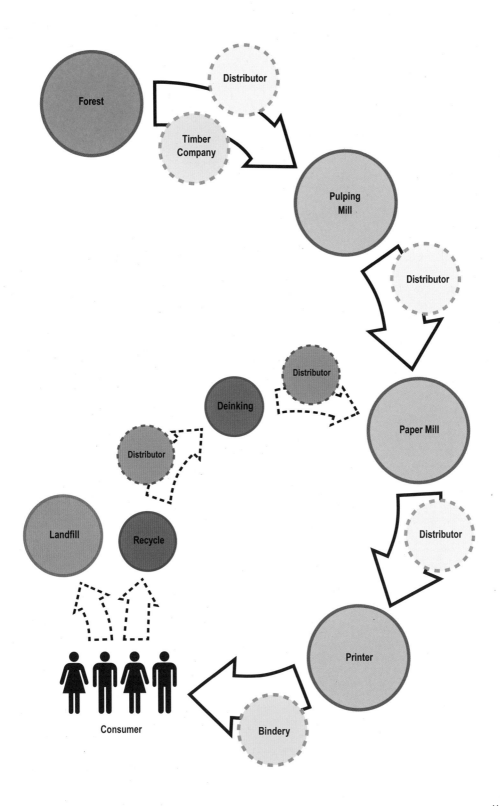

Deforestation in the Amazon can be the result of local people's need for agricultural land. Sustainable forestry practices can help provide the means for local communities to make a living off of forest resources.

It is no secret in the print and paper trade that the role graphic designers play is incredibly important. I know this to be true, and I believe the responsibility for environmental progress rests heavily with the design community.

DEREK SMITH – environmental paper consultant

FORESTRY

As the first step in the lifecycle of paper, commercial forestry and environmental management have an important role to play in a designers' abilities to work sustainably. One of the most common misconceptions that people have about forestry is that planting new trees is equivalent to saving forests. That is simply not the case. In the United States, millions of new trees are planted each year, and annual plantings actually exceed the number of trees cut for industrial purposes. However, these plantations do not have the same benefits as natural forests.

Old growth forests, which includes boreal and rainforests, are forests that have been allowed to grow naturally for more than 100 years and have developed into complete ecosystems containing every stage of tree life as well as the appropriate bio-diversity of other plants and animals. Intact forests have not been significantly disturbed by fire, logging, clear cutting, road building, or other human activity. The difference in the environmental and societal benefits of plantation tracks versus old growth forests are enormous, and around the world community groups, nongovernmental organizations (NGOs), and governmental organizations are working to minimize the destruction to the remaining intact forests.

Forest Facts	The following facts are from a presentation put together by George Milner, senior vice president of environmental affairs at Mohawk Paper:
	1. The countries emitting the most carbon into the atmosphere from tropical deforestation are Brazil, Indonesia, Burma, Mexico, and Thailand.
	2. Tree plantations host about 90 percent fewer species than the forests that preceded them.[2]
	3. About 71 percent of the world's paper supply is not made from timber harvested at tree farms but from forest-harvested timber, from regions with ecologically valuable, biologically diverse habitat.[3]
	4. The impact the paper industry has on land use (deforestation primarily in tropical rainforests) currently constitutes about 30 percent of CO_2 emissions traceable to human activity. At least 37.5 million acres of rainforests are lost annually.[4]

Forestry and Global Warming

Though protection of natural habitats and endangered species are compelling arguments for sustainable forestry, the emergence of global climate change as a pivotal issue has led to an increased focus on preservation of old growth forests. Intact forestlands act like giant natural carbon traps (storing between 62 and 78 percent of terrestrial biospheric carbon, which is more than any other ecosystem) and the destruction and deforestation of these areas releases large amounts of CO_2 into the atmosphere. In addition to the carbon dioxide that trees take in, the rich organic matter found in forests (including fallen branches, leaves, and rich soil) stores CO_2 as long as it remains undisturbed. Each year an area of tropical forests equivalent to the size of New York state are felled and burned. CO_2 emissions generated by deforestation make up 20 percent of the annual total, a fact that only intensifies the need for responsibly sourced forest products. It would be unfair to blame commercial logging for all occurrences of deforestation. In some cases forests are cut and burned so that native populations can use the land for agricultural purposes, and the growing demand for land by urbanized populations also contributes to the destruction of natural forest habitats.

Why Tree Fiber Is Still Needed

It might seem that discontinuing the use of virgin fiber (fiber that comes directly from its organic source) in paper production would be the best way to combat deforestation and illegal logging. Unfortunately, there is not enough recycled waste paper to satisfy global demands nor has any other agricultural crop proved to be a viable alternative to fiber from wood sources. For the foreseeable future, there will continue to be a need for forest products from virgin sources.

Clear cutting leaves a devastated landscape. It destroys habitat for native animals and exposed ground increases the risk of soil erosion.

Sustainable Forestry

If conducted in a sustainable manner, the impacts of commercial forestry can be greatly reduced. Sustainable forestry is a management system that works to maintain a full range of economic societal and environmental values. Choosing paper and timber products from sustainably managed forests that are independently certified using a chain of custody system is the best way for graphic designers to support the environmental and social systems that are found in healthy forests.

What is Sustainable Forestry According to Rainforest Alliance

Sustainable forestry provides a way of using trees and non-timber forest products to meet people's ever-increasing need for lumber, paper, and other products, without degrading forest ecosystems. Sustainable forestry is a process by which companies adopt more responsible practices: They increase protection of soils, waterways, and wildlife, and they treat workers and neighboring communities fairly. Sustainable forestry ensures that forestlands retain their economic value for the long term.[5]

Look for products with Forest Stewardship Council (FSC) certifications on the label, such as this Domtar paper. Domtar's forests are certified through Rainforest Alliance's Smart Wood program.

PHOTO COURTESY OF RAINFOREST ALLIANCE
AND DOMTAR PAPER

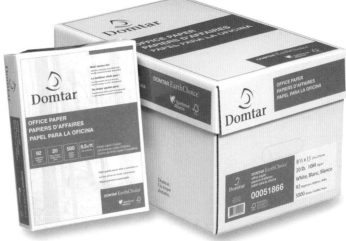

Over the past thirteen years, more than ninety million hectares in more than eighty-two countries have been certified according to Forestry Stewardship Council (FSC) standards while several thousand products are produced using FSC-certified wood and carrying the FSC trademark. FSC operates through its network of national initiatives in forty-three countries.

FORESTRY STEWARDSHIP COUNCIL

Chain of Custody

"Chain of custody" refers to a system of reporting and assessment used to verify that a product has been properly handled and produced, from its origins to the consumer. Essentially a tracking system, chain of custody certifications and reports usually occur in writing and are independently checked by third party organizations with experts who can ensure that a company or product meets specified criteria. In addition to markings or labels that may be put onto a product, the certifying body can provide documentation that a product or service has been tracked (in the case of paper from sustainably managed forests) and meets the requirements that the organization or certifying body stipulates.

FSC

While numerous trade organizations and governmental bodies may regulate or certify forest products, the most respected and widely recognized international certification body is the Forest Stewardship Council (FSC). FSC uses accredited third party certifiers to assess the environmental performance of manufacturers, distributors, retailers, and printers against FSC's performance standards. Using a chain of custody system, FSC bases its assessment on ten principles and criteria for forest management that were developed collaboratively by foresters, forestry companies, consumer and retail companies, environmental and social organizations, and community forestry groups. FSC works with partners around the world to ensure that forest ecosystems remain intact even after an area is logged. It does not certify large-scale logging practices such as clear cutting.

The Need for Sustainable Forestry

Rainforest Alliance works with businesses, local communities, and governmental organizations to promote responsible forest practices. Through its accrediting body, Smart Wood, Rainforest Alliance works in fifty-eight countries as a certifier for FSC and tries to increase global demand for certified forest products.

Liza Murphy, senior manager of marketing and business development at Rainforest Alliance, says that with sustainable forestry, "one can enhance the economic value of a forest by minimizing the environmental impacts and enhancing the social good." She says that FSC is an improvement over other certifications. "There is no other standard that is as vigorous," she says, "FSC is the standard; it is global and has truly integrated the social component in sustainable forestry." Rainforest Alliance helps small community-based enterprises participate in the FSC certification system and enter the global marketplace.

Murphy underscores that, "If you are talking about sustainability, you aren't just talking about the environment." When asked about the higher price premiums that sometimes go with FSC certified or postconsumer recycled paper, Murphy says that for the most part, "The price premium has mostly gone away. However, once FSC paper ends up at the market price, noncertified producers will have pressure to bring prices down." If makers of noncertified paper lower prices, then FSC may still end up costing more. Murphy says, "Price is only an issue in the absence of value," and that certified products "bring peace of mind."

Over the past three years, we have found many supporters for our approach to working ethically on paper-sourcing, from our illustrators and authors, to customers and staff. It's exciting to know that we are now sharing the Egmont Paper Grading System with like-minded publishing houses through the formation of PREPS; after all that is the truly ethical thing to do!

CALLY POPLAK – director, Egmont Press

Certifications and Environmental Labeling

Without proper labeling and certification, it is difficult, if not impossible, for consumers to know whether they are really getting environmentally preferable products. Independent third party certification is the most reliable way for manufacturers and customers to make responsible purchasing decisions. Certifications such as the International Organization for Standardization's (ISO), and the European Union's Eco-Management and Audit Scheme (EMAS), FSC, and Green e provide guarantees that products or manufacturing processes meet a strict set of criteria. Though well-meaning industry trade groups make information available to consumers, it is easy to overlook or be confused by data and/or advice that comes from organizations with ties to industry. Meredith Christiansen, product manager at Neenah Paper, says that businesses are just as happy to have certifications as consumers. "Third party certifiers help level the playing field," she explains. "They ensure that everyone is measuring themselves against the same standards, and they provide customers with a way to assess quality and measure our products against someone else's." Once you become familiar with the most common eco-labels and certifications, it is easy to investigate which systems most closely fit the criteria that you and your client are targeting.

International Organization of Standards (ISO)	ISO is a non-governmental organization made up of a network of the national standards institutes of 157 countries, which all participate in the development of international market-driven standards for industry.
	ISO 9000 and 14000 are quality and environmental management standards that a company may choose to adopt. A company's performance is evaluated against ISO's conformity assessment. ISO 9000 means that the organization in question has committed to enhance customer satisfaction by meeting customer and applicable regulatory requirements. ISO 14000 is a family of certifications that mean that the organization or company is committed to minimizing the harmful effects on the environment caused by its activities and continually improving its environmental performance. www.iso.org

Chlorine Free Products Association
Chlorine Free Products Association (CFPA) is a certification program for companies that produce chlorine free products. A product bearing the Totally Chlorine Free (TCF) or Processed Chlorine Free (PCF) emblem is subject to ongoing testing, inspection, and enforcement. www.chlorinefreeproducts.org

Processed Chlorine Free
The Processed Chlorine Free (PCF) seal is reserved for paper that includes recycled fibers that meet Environmental Protection Agency guidelines for recycled or postconsumer content and have not been rebleached with chlorine containing compounds. Minimum of 30 percent postconsumer content is required.

EMAS
The European Union Eco-Management and Audit Scheme (EMAS) is a management tool for companies and other organizations to evaluate, report, and improve their environmental performance. www.ec.europa.eu/environment/emas

Green e
The Green e logo identifies products made by companies that purchase certified renewable energy to offset a portion or all of their electricity use. Renewable energy types include but are not limited to wind power, solar power, low impact hydropower, and biomass. www.green-e.org

Green Seal
Green Seal is an independent nonprofit organization dedicated to safeguarding the environment and transforming the marketplace by promoting manufacture, purchase, and use of environmentally responsible products and services. www.greenseal.org

FSC
Forest Stewardship Council (FSC) is a nonprofit international organization which promotes the responsible forest management. Products carrying the FSC label are independently certified they come from forests that are managed to meet the social, economic, and ecological needs of present and future generations. www.fsc.org

The Spanish Forest in Ontario, Canada

Based in Montreal, Canada, Domtar is the largest producer of uncoated freesheet papers in North America and a leading manufacturer of pulp. Launched in 2005, Domtar's EarthChoice line is supported with logos from the FSC and Rainforest Alliance. The management practices for thirteen million of the company's twenty-two million acres of forestland in Canada and the United States are certified by the FSC. Since Domtar controls both forests and paper production it can transparently track its products from tree to consumer. The company works ahead of regulations and with NGO's to continually increase the percentage of its forests that are sustainably managed, and is therefore able to offer more environmentally-preferable products to consumers.

Road trip host Marc Trottier (left), operations forester for the Spanish Forest and author of the 2005-2025 Spanish Forest Management Plan, with Lewis Fix (center), director of business development-corporate markets, and Keith Ley, policy and planning analyst (right). As part of a regulated process of road building, cutting, and replanting, Trottier Ley and Fix are part of a team that works to ensure that the Spanish Forest is being sustainably maintained for current use and future generations.

Spanish Forest in Ontario, Canada

Domtar's commitment to sustainability was reinforced when the company observed a shift in the marketplace from tangible to intangible value. Lewis C. Fix, director of business development at Domtar says that seeing other companies' stocks plummet due to social or environmental challenges was a wake-up for many corporations and prompted Domtar to analyze its own supply chain for similar risks. The company found that independently certifying its facilities and forestry practices was the best way to mitigate risk and gain access to new markets. Subsequently, Domtar developed a relationship with Monte Hummel, president of World Wildlife Fund-Canada (WWF), which led to a signed commitment to work with WWF and Rainforest Alliance (an FSC accrediting body) to certify that all of Domtar's forest holdings were being sustainably managed. Fix has observed that even in the past two and a half years there has been an increased demand for its FSC-certified products, and the company has responded by doubling the number of grades in the product line that carry FSC certification. "When we have enough fiber, we prefer to convert a whole product line but when we don't have enough we convert what we can," Fix says. "Either way, we keep the products priced competitively."

FSC Paper Made by Domtar	Tons of FSC-certified paper produced by Domtar, per year. 2004: 40,000 2005: 100,000 2006: 120,000 2007: 300,000

A recent cut illustrates the residual trees left for wildlife as required by Ontario Ministry of Natural Resource's "National Disturbance Pattern Emulation Guidelines." These residuals meet FSC requirements for individual residual trees as well.

After timber was harvested, the site was prepared and seeded from the air for regeneration of the jack pine forest. The seed to regenerate these sites is obtained by cone collectors from the tops of trees felled on cuts. To help to maintain natural genetic adaptations in regenerating forest stands, the seed or planting stock produced from the harvested cones is returned to the original ecological seed zone. Seedling production for planted sites is contracted out to established growers.

Tom Kaboni, a feller-buncher operator, leaves residual trees on the cuts "for the birds" according to the guidelines developed by the FSC and Ontario Ministry of Natural Resources.

Egmont UK Grading System

When Egmont UK, the second largest publisher of children's books in the United Kingdom, was asked where the paper used to print their books came from, they found that the issue was more complicated than they anticipated. An evaluation of Egmont's paper sourcing found that a single sheet used in one of Egmont's many titles, could contain several pulps, each of which might have been sourced from forests in different parts of the world.

In 2003, the company partnered with environmental consultants Acona to create the Egmont Grading System, a tool that was designed to help eliminate Egmont's use of papers containing fiber from questionable or illegal sources. Egmont asked their suppliers (mostly printers) to evaluate the stocks that were used to print Egmont's products with the new grading system. Sam Mawson, project controller at Egmont says, "We decided that evolution rather than revolution was the best way to approach the issue. Keeping our key print suppliers on board was vital to the success of the project. Anything too immediate would have jeopardized their support." Nevertheless, Egmont made it clear that compliance and cooperation were a must. "We explained to them that this was the way we were moving and that if they wanted to continue to work with us then they would have to be on board. Since this issue had been around for a while, most of our key suppliers were thankful that someone was offering them a solution." In addition to only using papers that reached at least a grade 3 on the scale, Egmont also began to print a small but increasing number of titles on FSC-certified or recycled stock.

In June 2007, Alison Kennedy, Egmont's production director, approached a number of fellow U.K. publishers to explore the idea of working together to increase the use of preferential paper in the industry. In September 2007, Publishers database for Responsible Environmental Paper Sourcing (PREPS) was formed with a coalition of companies that together make up 35 percent of the publishing market in the U.K. Using the grading system originally developed by Acona and Egmont, PREPS provides members with objective information about paper through a web-based, password enabled database. Simon Thresh, senior partner at Acona, explains, "The intention is for PREPS to make life easier for everyone, with less duplication of effort by members and more consistency in the questions that are being asked of printers, merchants, and paper companies."

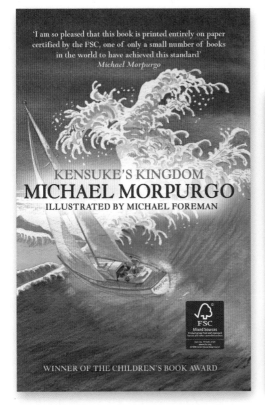

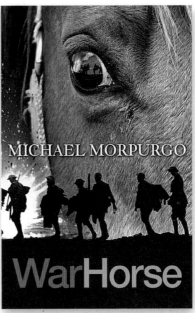

Egmont uses eco-labels to educate consumers about the papers used in the production of its children's books.

Egmont Paper Grading System

Egmont grades paper using a 1 to 5 criteria system, the company will only purchase paper that receives a grade of 3 or above. In 2006, Egmont used approximately 5,000 tons of paper, of that amount 70 percent was a grade 3 or 4, and 30 percent was grade 5.

5: Meets FSC requirements and can be labeled as such

4: Includes FSC and recycled content but may require effort to be labeled

3: All material is sourced from legal origins with reasonable amounts of data

2: Source of material is under review and/or there is insufficient data

1: Unknown or suspect material from unwanted sources

For the full Egmont Paper Grading Guide or for full explanation of how the company grades paper, refer to the "Egmont Paper Purchasing Standard" at www.egmont.com.

PAPER PRODUCTION

In its 1999 report, Environmental Defense (through their Paper Working Group) identified pulp and paper manufacturing as the step in the lifecycle of paper that is responsible for the majority of the material's negative environmental impacts.[7] Paper and pulp mills transform cellulose fiber (either logs or chips) into finished paper products. This manufacturing process needs thousands of gallons of water per ton of finished material, it uses chemicals to break-down the wood into useable fibers, and these processes all require an enormous amount of energy. Motivated by legislation, consumer pressure, and the desire to become more efficient, the pulp and paper industry in the United States has heavily invested in new technologies and processes that reduce its environmental impact. Even though the industry has made progress in the past twenty-five years, paper production continues to be a focal point for people who want to practice eco-friendly print production. There are opportunities to minimize or eliminate the environmental impacts during each step in the paper-making process.

Paper Production Target Areas
- Wood used in production (see sections on Forestry and Recycled Papers)
- Water and air (usage and potential contamination)
- Chemicals used in bleaching
- Energy consumption
- Safe working conditions for employees

Companies practicing sustainable paper production should minimize the use of natural resources, target pollution prevention (not just control), and have an articulated environmental management system that sets company-wide targets. Manufacturers should actively work to minimize the impact that the paper production process has on the ecological and social systems surrounding their facilities while providing a clean and safe environment for workers.

A Mohawk Fine Paper employee checking the quality of a roll of newly made paper

How Paper Is Made

Paper production begins when raw materials (usually logs or wood chips) are pulped to produce useable fiber. Wood is broken down in two common ways, and each method has environmental benefits and disadvantages.

Chemical pulping (referred to as the Kraft process) is the most common method used to produce fiber for fine papers (such as those specified for most design jobs). Wood chips are mixed with chemicals and water and then heated under pressure to break down the fibers and dissolve the lignin. Chemical pulping uses less energy than mechanical pulping, but it also produces less usable fiber per ton of raw material. Mills that want to maximize efficiency may burn waste from the Kraft process, called black liquor, to produce steam that is used to run the mill.

Mechanical pulping uses force and sometimes heat (as in thermomechanical pulping) to break down fibers and separate lignin (a glue-like substance that binds wood fibers together) and wood sugar from the useable fibers. This method uses fewer chemicals and a smaller number of trees to yield the same amount of pulp as the Kraft process but it uses far more energy.

Labeling is an important part of a chain of custody system. Here an instrument called a dandy puts the FSC watermark directly on a wet Neenah Paper sheet so it is distinguishable as FSC-certified.

After pulping, fibers are washed to remove impurities and lignin. They are then bleached several times to obtain the brightness required by white papers. Most industrialized countries—including the European Union, the United States, and Canada—have passed environmental legislation that requires companies to minimize or eliminate the use of materials that produce volatile organic compounds (VOCs—see Glossary, page 186) that are associated with chemicals such as elemental chlorine, which were traditionally used in the bleaching process. In the past twenty years, the industry has moved from the use of elemental chlorine to chlorine dioxide or to totally chlorine free bleaching using ozone or hydrogen peroxide. Designers concerned about the environmental effects of bleaching should look for paper products that are elemental or totally chlorine free or specify sheets that are less white.

Next, refined and bleached fiber is suspended in water (in a mixture called furnish) and run onto fabric or wire where fibers form a mat of paper from which water is extracted using both heat and pressure. In the case of coated stock, sizing is sprayed onto the sheet to help ink adhere to paper and to keep it from soaking through. These coatings may contain minerals such those found in stone or clay or they can be made from renewable materials such as cornstarch. The additives used in different paper products vary enough that it is best to ask your distributor or printer to find out how environmentally conscious a paper company is during this part of the process. Paper is ironed, polished, and wound onto spools before it is sent to distributors.

Energy Usage

Paper production is an energy intensive process. Mills consume about 31 million BTUs of energy to produce one ton of paper or paperboard.[8] Energy consumption is one of the main areas to target when one is specifying environmentally friendly paper products. Some mills can make their own power from waste generated during the pulping process. (This may be considered "renewable," but ask about air pollution if waste burning is part of the process.) Other companies have programs to purchase energy from renewable sources. Renewable energy is a good alternative to power generated from nuclear or fossil fuel sources. Where and how a mill obtains the energy it uses and whether there are conservation programs in place can be an important way of assessing a company's commitment to reducing its environmental impact.

The very largest paper mills can take in sawn logs at one side of the plant and deliver finished rolls of paper out the other, but not all paper companies engage in the full production process. Jeff Mendelsohn, president of New Leaf Paper, saw an industry where there was immense potential to make positive change. New Leaf Paper doesn't make its own paper. The company mostly works in research and development and contracts with mills to find ways of producing better paper. New Leaf Paper has helped to drive the market for eco-friendly paper by constantly raising the bar and making paper that has an ultra-high percentage of postconsumer waste, uses chlorine free bleaching, and includes non-wood fibers. Mendelsohn notes, "Markets reward companies that make better decisions." He believes that a company should have a "core benefit of doing something good, strengthen value of the brand, and reflect well on staffing and people who work at the company." At $25 million a year in sales, New Leaf Paper may be a small player by international standards, but the company is still doing a lot of business. New Leaf Paper serves a niche market that values excellence in performance and wants the most environmentally preferable paper available.

Every day the Neenah Paper mill generates a full container of dried sludge similar to the one seen in this photograph.

Recycling and Reuse at Neenah Paper

By recycling or using the waste they generate, Neenah Paper has created a closed loop system of paper production and virtually eliminated the need for landfill waste disposal at their Neenah, Wisconsin mill.

Neenah Paper contracts with Industrial Recyclers of Wisconsin (IROW) for disposal of its industrial waste. Dotted throughout the mill are recycling containers of all sizes where scrap, metal, containers, and other materials that can't be remanufactured into new paper can be collected. IROW picks up collected material and turns it into a variety of useable goods.

Like many facilities, Neenah Paper previously used a boiler to generate the steam needed to power the mill and dry paper. Today the mill's boiler idles zero, and the company now uses "green steam," which is produced using the mill's own sludge. Sludge is a bi-product of paper production. It contains materials that were unable to be used to produce paper such as dirt, dye, and fibers that are too weak to be made into paper. At the Neenah Paper mill, sludge is collected, dried, and sent to Fox Valley Energy Center, a local clean incineration facility. There the sludge is burned to produce "green steam" and a glass aggregate that is used in asphalt and roof shingles. The steam generated at Fox Valley is sent back to Neenah Paper and is used to power the mill.

Common Sources of Renewable Energy	Solar wind, Landfill gas, Bio mass, Geothermal, Low impact hydro
	In many cases, for a cost premium of less than 15 percent, customers in the United States can keep their current energy supplier but make stipulations that energy be purchased directly from renewable sources.

Sustainability is basically about doing the right thing.

ANN WILLOUGHBY – founder of the Willoughby Design Group

The Strathmore Sustainability Portfolio

When Mohawk Fine Papers reformatted its Strathmore Collection to be more eco-friendly, the company asked Willoughby Design Group in Kansas City to create a printed piece to showcase the product. Company founder Ann Willoughby saw the project as a great opportunity to use sustainable practices while creating an interesting and informative communications piece. By telling stories about six innovative sustainable brands and company initiatives, the Strathmore Sustainability Portfolio educates designers about sustainable thinking while serving as an example of environmentally responsible print production.

"We looked for one example of what was sustainable within a company—something in their marketing line, postcards, labels, stationery, etc. and produced something useful with the Strathmore line," said Willloughby. The printed pieces were bound into the portfolio so that designers could see examples of the new paper in action.

Describing the work of companies who are passionate about social and environmental responsibility was incredibly gratifying, but Willoughby believed that it was also important to create a printed piece that would impress designers. Proof that the portfolio met that goal came when several designers looked at it and commented, "I can't believe that this was sustainably made." Willoughby suggests that there are opportunities for everyone to make a difference, but there are real challenges as well. "I don't believe we can make this transition without cooperation and networking; you can't do it by yourself," she says.

The portfolio was printed primarily on Strathmore Script, 100 percent postconsumer waste, which is made carbon neutral by offsetting both the electrical and thermal energy used in the production process. The paper is certified by FSC, GreenSeal, and Green e.

Collateral pieces from each of the six companies profiled were printed with Strathmore papers and bound into the portfolio.

I am astonished to hear most people think soy inks are 100 percent soy based. More often, the content is about 14 percent soy based and 86 percent oil based.

GREG BARBER — an environmental print consultant, says that one of the most common misconceptions about ink is the amount of soy in "soy-based ink."

PRINTING

Printers can be key partners in the quest to adopt sustainable production practices. Historically, printing has been considered a dirty and even unhealthy business. However, innovations in technology and materials combined with governmental regulations have made significant strides toward cleaning up print production. Because printers are often the connection point between designers/customers and complicated manufacturing and production processes, they have an enormous responsibility to provide accurate information while maintaining clean and efficient facilities. By working with printers that constantly strive to reduce their impact on the environment, designers can help encourage the industry to move in a more positive direction, while reaping the rewards of guilt-free printing.

Fast Steps To Greener Printing

What you can do

- Minimize paper use by specifying lighter-weight paper, using both sides, and designing with standard sizes to get the most out of each sheet.
- Choose paper that is totally chlorine free with high postconsumer recycled content or that is FSC certified.
- Avoid neon and metallic inks.
- Use water-based, non-chlorinated glues and coatings.
- Avoid printing more than you need.
- Specify the use of waterless lithography when possible.

What your printer can do

- Use the most environmentally preferable inks and cleaners with low or no VOCs.
- Have programs in place to reduce water and energy use.
- Recycle as much as possible.
- Safely dispose of waste.

The Myth of Soy Ink

In the 1980s, the American Soybean Association began to look for ways of promoting materials and processes that utilized soy. Replacing petroleum or other vegetable-based inks was one of their initiatives, and in 1993 the National Soy Ink Information Center was established by the Iowa Soybean Association to advertise the benefits of soy ink. A SoySeal trademark was designed and printers and ink manufacturers were encouraged to use the mark to visually promote a product that claimed to be environmentally preferable because it used a renewable crop and was easier to recycle. The newspaper industry was quick to adopt soy over petroleum-based inks, and by the year 2000 about 90 percent of American newspapers were printing using ink with some percentage of soybean oil.

The overwhelming success of the American Soybean Association's campaign was not a sizeable step forward for environmental preferable printing. The truth is that inks containing a similar percentage of vegetable oil had been in use for more than a century, and petroleum-based inks came into vogue on the heels of a similar public relations campaign by the petrochemical industry decades before. Soy ink is not inherently better than ink using other vegetable-based oils, and the misleading public relations campaign by the National Soy Ink Information Center made it seem like specing environmentally preferable inks was as simple as choosing soy. Richard Snyder of Great Western Ink says, "Print buyers today should not just be concerned with the use of soy oil (unless you have a vested interest in growing soybeans). They should ask if their printer is doing their part to reduce VOCs, monitoring their waste streams, using vegetable-based ink etc, or, in other words, are they printing green?"

Reality Check	Environmental groups suggest specifying non-soy vegetable-based ink. Liza Murphy, senior manager of marketing and business development at Rainforest Alliance, underscores this point by explaining that, "Planting soybeans is the single biggest cause of Amazon deforestation."

Offset Lithography

Offset lithography accounts for the vast majority of printed material that is produced and should be the first area of production targeted by graphic designers who want to improve their environmental footprints. It is a complicated process that may use toxic or unhealthy materials, it requires a great deal of energy, and it generates waste that must be properly disposed of. Fortunately, materials such as vegetable-based inks and citrus-based cleanup solutions as well as the use of processes such as waterless lithography that can mitigate many of the negative effects of offset printing and should become part of production specifications for graphic designers who want to adopt sustainable practices.

VOCs

VOCs are fumes emitted from solvents, inks, and cleaners used in the printing process. Prolonged exposure to VOCs can have negative effects on a person's health, and VOCs are a major contributor to ozone in the lower atmosphere. In recent years, companies have introduced products that have significantly reduced or even eliminated the VOCs emitted by inks, solvents, and press washes. Insync Marketing Solutions, an environmentally conscious printer in Los Angeles, California, uses the Liberty sheetfed inks by Sun Chemical (sold under the Kohl & Madden brand). Liberty inks generate less waste, produce great color, and the manufacturer has removed VOCs, making Liberty one of the most environmentally sound options on the market today.

The vast majority of printed material is produced using offset lithography.

Ink

Ink is made by combining pigments, binders (which help pigment adhere to paper), and a vehicle that is used to hold and carry the pigment. Vegetable oil (e.g., cottonseed, linseed, or soy), petroleum, and water all can be used as a vehicle in different kinds of ink. While the benefits of soy were exaggerated, vegetable-based inks do tend to release fewer VOCs than petroleum-based inks and are also easier to de-ink during paper recycling. Water-based inks (see Waterless Printing, page 74) are better for the environment than either those containing petroleum or vegetable oil. They emit no VOCs and are easier to clean up, but because they are not in wide use, they probably won't be an option for most jobs.

Pigments are added to ink to produce color and have traditionally contained heavy metals such as barium, copper, and zinc. These metals pose a risk to employees who may suffer health problems from long-term exposure. The metals also contribute to ground water contamination, both in waste from the printing facilities and also in landfills where most printed paper ends up. Due to regulation and research, many of the worst metals have been removed from ink recipes, but asking a printer about which colors contain the fewest heavy metals is still important.

Cleaning and Solvents

Press equipment and blankets have to be cleaned between runs, and there are many environmentally preferable cleaning solutions available to do the job. One option is citrus-based solutions. (Think of a more concentrated version of CITRA-Solv that one might use in the home.) These work just as well at removing ink from a press as solvent-based solutions. However they are not perfect in every situation. Printers should chose a product based on their equipment, the inks they use, and the press operator's preference.

Water

The printing industry as a whole, with the exception of digital printing and waterless lithography, uses large amounts of water on press either directly or as ingredients in dampening solutions. Printers can use waterless lithography or closed loop systems where waste water (or solutions) is collected and recycled or safely processed and disposed of.

Finishing and Binding

UV coatings and glue bindings are favorite techniques of designers, but until recently they have been frowned on by environmentalists. It is now possible to get UV coatings that are 100 percent water based and nontoxic. These coatings are not widely available, so your printer should be prepared to do a bit of searching. There have also been improvements in glues and binding options. However folds and/or staples are still preferable because they tend to be easier to remove during recycling. Other environmentally friendly options, such as embossing and diecutting, can help a designer achieve a polished look with minimal environmental impact.

Proper disposal of printing wastes involves a wide range of processes and specialized equipment. Recycling and disposal equipment is housed both in and outside the plant.

Anderson Lithography

Los Angeles–based Anderson Lithography has a fifteen-year history of implementing the highest levels of environmental principles and practices. Through an evolution of policies and procedures for handling printing waste by-products, the company has eliminated the need to send waste to landfills. "We will not send any hazardous or non-hazardous waste by-product to any landfill—period!" the company states.

Anderson Lithography is FSC certified and was the 2003 recipient of the South Coast Air Quality Management District's Clean Air Award for their innovative use of their Cogeneration on-site power plant and integrated heating, ventilating, and air-conditioning systems to capture and destroy all "fugitive" volatile organic compound emissions. On their website, www.andlitho.com, Anderson Lithograph makes available extensive documentation about their sustainable policies and practices as well as useful information about what to ask printers and how print buyers can work more sustainably.

Paper is not the only waste generated by printers; there are also ink and solvent containers, glues, and contaminated water, all of which need to be safely disposed of.[9] Most printers recycle the paper waste generated during printing because, in addition to being environmentally preferable, it creates a small revenue stream. Ask your printer if they have programs to dispose of all the industrial waste their facility generates. Most of it can be recycled, reused, or even composted. After years of commitment to a clean, safe press room, Anderson Lithography has managed to eliminate landfill waste from their operations. If they can do it then others can, too.

The 2006 Toshiba annual report used waterless printing that was certified by the Waterless Printing Association.

Waterless Printing

Waterless printing offers significant advantages even when compared with other environmentally conscious offset printing. Unlike conventional offset lithography—a chemical process that requires water and dampening solutions—waterless printing uses a specific temperature range to transfer ink to the substrate. The elimination of water—and fountain solutions that contain isopropyl alcohol or their substitutes—vastly reduces the water used and VOCs emitted on press. Waterless printing is also more efficient; printers that have switched to waterless printing report increased productivity of more than 100 percent. Unfortunately, so few printers offer this service that there is a great deal of misunderstanding about the technology. The truth is that waterless is cost effective and can be used to produce everything that would be printed with traditional offset lithography.

Arthur Lefebvre, executive director of the Waterless Printing Association, believes that the adoption of waterless technology by U.S. printers has been held up for two reasons. First, an insufficient supply of the specially made plates that are used in the process. Second is the lack of skilled press operators who will take the time to understand the delicate temperature balance required for waterless printing. Lefebvre says that printers who devote the resources to switching systems report significant savings to the environment while increasing output. "Take one 40-inch sheet-fed press running 5 or 6 colors," says Lefebvre. "In one year, approximately 3,100 to 3,700 gallons of water are saved and 320 to 425 gallons of fountain solution are eliminated." Waterless printing has been more readily adopted in Japan—where Toray, a main supplier of plates, is located—and in other countries where there are incentives for reducing VOCs. Waterless lithography will likely become more popular in the U.S. as concern for fresh water resources intensifies and polluting industries come under greater scrutiny.

Digital Printing

Digital printing is usually considered environmentally preferable for jobs requiring fewer than 2,000 copies. It is also a good option for larger pieces such as signage or banners. Digital printing includes toner-based printers such as Laser printers, which use heat to adhere dry pigment to paper, as well as ink jet systems, which spray water and solvent-based ink directly onto paper or other printing material. Digital printing is environmentally preferable because toner inks don't use any alcohol or emit VOCs, and even ink jet printing has virtually eliminated off-gassing.

One of the main benefits of digital printing is that it doesn't require messy cleanup. Some companies have programs that allow used ink cartridges and other printing waste (such as printer components and used ink depositories) to be returned to the manufacturer for recycling. In the case of ink-jet printing, there are new environmentally friendly papers, manmade and natural, that can be run in both small and wide-format printers.

Commenting on Xerox Corporation's announcement of the launch of the iGen3 Green Machine, Frank Romano, former administrative chair of Rochester Institute of Technology's School of Printing Management and Sciences says, "The printing industry has made remarkable improvements in waste management. By applying digital printing, [the printing industry] is using a more efficient reproduction process that does not require startup waste and creates virtually no disposal problems."

Tough Questions

A dramatic increase in demand for green printing has caused some printers to claim to be eco-friendly or green when in reality they have made very few changes other than re-branding their companies. Shops that have made the most significant strides toward sustainable printing are not always the ones that advertise the loudest. Look for independent certifications. These can be expensive and out of the range for small shops, but talking to a printer with FSC and ISO 14000 certification (and EMAS in Europe) is likely to be an eye-opening experience. Remember, a printer may use FSC-certified paper without being certified themselves. (This is often a good option for smaller companies.)

By asking a few questions about eco-friendly ink and press cleanup, any savvy designer will get the sense of whether the person they talk to is being evasive. It's not unusual to hear, "Printing has always been a dirty business, and even with improvements it still is," or "Are you sure you really want eco-friendly printing? It costs a lot more." Neither of these statements are necessarily true. When you get responses like this, move on and don't be afraid to tell a shop that you are taking your business elsewhere because another company offers better environmental options or is more competitively priced. Salespeople report that customer demands often make it easier to convince shop owners to adopt better practices. (Note that this is true only for printing in North America and Europe. There tend to be fewer options in developing countries, and environmentally responsible printing there may be out of range in the short term. See page 66 for tips on working sustainably even without green printing.)

The Low-Down on Cost

There is a lot of disagreement about whether or not environmentally responsible printing really costs more. The answer is both yes and no. It really depends on the kind of jobs you do and type of printing that you compare it against. If a designer is used to cheap imported paper at rock bottom prices (with somewhat questionable quality) to begin with, or prints overseas where labor costs are minimal, then the answer is yes, your client may have to pay a small premium for green printing. On the other hand, if you are used to relatively high-quality printing, it is usually possible to find similar or better service at the same price, in North America and Europe. Look for experienced printers who stock environmentally responsible paper for their house sheets (some percentage of FSC or PCW recycled content) and/or have preferential purchasing relationships with paper companies.

FSC CERTIFIED PULP   RECYCLED WASTE   **MIXED SOURCES** | BEST PRICE OPTION

New Efforts from Chinese Printers

Reporting back from a trip to explore sustainable printing partnerships in China, Gary Gonzales, Rainmaker-Eco Solutions at Insync Marketing Solutions, found that the printing industry in China is taking note of an increase in demand for environmentally responsible printing.

Based in Los Angeles, Insync Marketing Solutions works as an intermediary for clients who are concerned about the environment, but either because of cost or quantity, don't feel that printing in the United States is a viable option. Whether printing sustainably or not, working with Chinese printers can have considerable cost benefits. Insync Marketing Solutions, which already offers environmentally responsible printing at their Los Angeles facility, believes that there is an emerging market in acting as a liaison between U.S. clients and FSC-certified Chinese printers.

Gonzales visited two of the ten printers with FSC certification in China. "Hung Hing and Elegance, both in Shenzhen province, are modern and well-kept facilities with seemingly content workers," Gonzales says. "We took note that they treat their employees well, and like most manufacturing business in China, the employees are housed, fed, and given medical attention at the plant."

Hoping to offer clients the best of both worlds, Insync Marketing Solutions has come up with a model where they will take responsibility for the prepress needed for materials produced by their Chinese partners. "That way we can control the color and graphic elements of the design," Gonzales says. "We are working on IT8 color profiles with our partners so our final color files can easily be matched in China."

Gonzales found that there are challenges beyond obvious language barriers when working with Chinese companies and believes that, for the foreseeable future, clients will be better served by working with intermediaries who have experience in the area. "I have heard from others who have worked in China that color control is difficult to maintain, and if there is too much back and forth with proofs, precious time is lost," says Gonzales. "We are building a model that will make working with Chinese printers more efficient while still offering costs savings and sustainable printing to our clients."

Hung Hing shows off their FSC certification with framed lists of credentials in their lobby

Finished product being inspected for quality

Image of plant workers taken in the 'hand' bindery department. The printer has more than twenty-five large printing presses, and it does work for companies such as Mattel and Disney. Just a part of the first floor is shown here. There are two floors just of hand labor with about 600 workers per shift.

Nelson Luis Smythe Jr.

Sustainable Print Production Gains Momentum in Brazil

by Nelson Luis Smythe Jr., graphic eco-designer and researcher at the Center of Design & Sustainability at the Universidade Federal do Paraná in Brazil

Sustainable development is part of the Brazilian enterprise agenda, and more companies are implanting systems of environment management to get certifications such as ISO 14000 and FSC as well as working toward other sustainable environmental processes. Brazilian graphic designers who are interested in practicing sustainably often employ general guidelines that are taken from the available literature on product design, which has more fully developed research in the country. These include the following:

- Decreasing the amount of raw material used
- Prioritizing resources by using renewable and local produced material
- Using green stamps for the identification of recycled products or materials
- Promoting the sustainable purchasing and the increasing of the useful life of the product

In 2006, as part of a newly launched sustainable agenda, unions for the printing industries of the Brazilian states São Paulo, Paraná, and Rio Grande do Sul, in partnership with the Abigraf (Brazilian Association of the Printing Industry) introduced the Manual Técnico-Ambiental da Indústria Gráfica (Technical-Environmental Manual of the Printing Industry). The manual was printed on recycled paper and designed by Aurus estúdio gráfico.

The most common step taken by graphic designers is still the use of recycled or FSC-certified paper and vegetable oil based-inks in printing. In October 2005, *As Intermitências da Morte*, by Jose Saramago, became the first book to be printed with FSC certification in Brazil. The Geographic Publishing Company (responsible for the impression of the book) was the first publishing company in Brazil to obtain the FSC label. Together the companies Suzano Paper and Cellulose (one of Latin America's largest producers of integrated pulp and paper and elemental chlorine free since 1986) launched an initiative so that more companies in the graphic industry could get the chain of custody FSC labeling. The project includes twenty-five printers, two manufacturers of notebooks, and three distributors of paper, all of which will initiate the certification process by 2008.

There is still work to be done toward the development of a methodology for integrating sustainable issues into practice and education so that Brazilian graphic designers can begin to include sustainability in project specifications. Ultimately the goal should be for designers to fully consider a project from conception through the discarding or final use of the product.

Livreto portfolio DESER— Departamento de Estudos Sócio-Econômicos Rurais (Portfolio booklet DESER—Department of Rural Socioeconomic Studies). 2004. Designed by Aurus estúdio gráfico. Printed on recycled paper.

RECYCLED PAPER

The quality of paper made from reclaimed waste material has risen steadily, and today a sheet of 100 percent recycled paper is indistinguishable from paper made with virgin fiber. The cost of using a sheet with recycled content varies, and paper that is 100 percent recycled may be somewhat more expensive than a similar product made from virgin pulp. However when one compares prices of paper produced from sustainably managed forests (like, FSC certified) with paper containing 100 percent recycled content, the costs are more comparable.

The Benefits of Recycled

Even though there has been some controversy about the benefits of using recycled versus virgin pulp, most environmental organizations and independent studies have concluded that there are clear benefits to recycling paper. The simplest way to think about the issue is that every sheet of paper that is reclaimed keeps material out of overflowing landfills.

Recycled Terminology

Labeling on paper that contains some percentage of reclaimed material can be confusing and even misleading. There are no regulations for when one may use the recycled logo, nor are there standards for what percentage of reclaimed content a product must have in order to be classified as recycled. Therefore, the term "recycled" can mean very different things to different manufacturers. When evaluating reclaimed paper, the most important distinction to make is between preconsumer and postconsumer waste.

What We Save	Conserveatree, a nonprofit organization dedicated to providing expert advice and leadership on paper choices, reports that one ton of recycled paper saves 3.3 cubic yards of landfill space. It also cites an Environmental Protection Agency study that estimates that a ton of 100 percent postconsumer recycled paper saves 7,000 gallons of water, 4,100 kilowatt hours of electricity, and 60 pounds of air pollution.

Other than the "recycled" logo, it is usually impossible to tell the difference between paper made with 100 percent postconsumer waste and that made with virgin fiber.

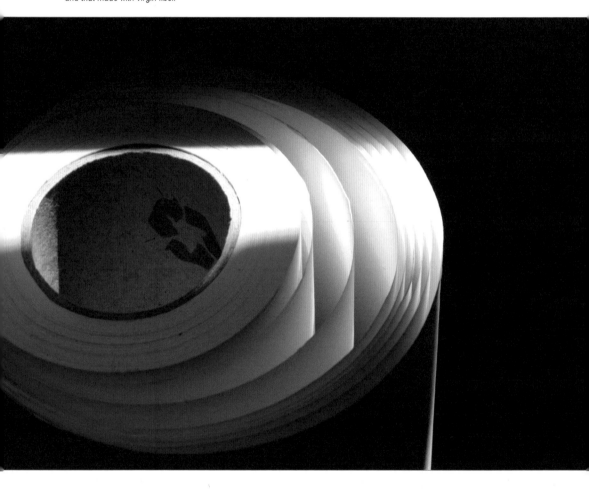

EPA Standards	The U.S. Environmental Protection Agency's own standards for paper in their offices require minimums of 30 percent postconsumer content for uncoated papers and 10 percent for coated papers. This requirement is broad enough that one should be able to find a competitively-based sheet in this range, and it can be a good benchmark to shoot for.

Preconsumer waste refers to scraps and ends from the manufacturing process, as well as test sheets and over-runs from printers; both of which are collected and remanufactured into new paper.

Postconsumer waste refers to material that has reached the consumer, been used, and then is collected to make new product. It is postconsumer waste that people commonly think of when they want recycled paper. However, preconsumer waste is reported to make up 20 percent of the reclaimed content used in paper today. Copy paper often has some percentage (usually 10 to 30 percent) of recycled content, and unless otherwise specified, this labeling may simply indicate that mill waste is being fed back into the manufacturing process. While preconsumer waste is an important indication that mills are being efficient, it is vital that companies label products so consumers understand where reclaimed content comes from.

Recycled content is only part of specing paper from environmentally preferable sources. More sheets than ever before are being produced with a combination of recycled content and virgin fiber from sustainably managed forests. FSC's mixed source label can now include some recycled content and provides a great option at competitive prices.

The Life Span of Paper

The life span of organic fibers is limited, and generally paper can be recycled only up to six times. As paper goes through multiple de-inking and remanufacturing processes, the natural fibers begin to break, and they eventually become too short to be used to make new paper. The more times fibers have been reused, the lower the grade of paper that can be made from them and/or greater amounts of virgin fiber will need to be added to offset the lesser quality of the recycled content. Newsprint and cardboard can be produced with lower quality reclaimed material and are ideally suited for high percentages of recycled content.

Spotlight on the Process

After being collected, sorted, and bailed, paper is sent to a de-inking mill. Unwanted material is removed with the help of chemicals called surfactants, which help separate ink, adhesives, and other contaminants from paper fibers. The pulp is washed and (for white paper) bleached, usually with a product similar to hydrogen peroxide. Because hydrogen peroxide is used instead of chlorine derivatives, this bleaching is considered less harmful than the bleaching that's done to virgin fiber. For lower grade products such as paper towels, tissue, or packaging, pulp doesn't need to be bleached. Recycled pulp is dried and bailed in thick sheets before being sent to papermaking mills to be used to make a range of different products.

One of the main environmental concerns associated with the recycling process is sludge that consists of leftover materials from the de-inking process. Though some mills reprocess sludge for use as fertilizer, the practice is controversial because sludge and the resulting fertilizer often contain the heavy metals from ink. Since reclaimed material may have been printed before environmental regulations took effect, even materials that are banned for use today can show up in sludge. The safe collection and disposal of de-inking waste remains an important environmental concern. However when paper is de-inked, any toxic elements found in sludge are less likely to contaminate ground water supplies than if waste paper was sent directly to landfills.

Disappearing Ink	For its Japanese market, Toshiba has developed "disappearing ink," which can be used in office printers on paper that will be recycled. The ink can be removed easily from large quantities of paper using thermal processing and a specially developed decolorizer. Toshiba's process allows reclaimed fibers to be used up to ten times and this product is in the same price range as conventional printer ink.
	Unfortunately "disappearing ink" is currently available only in Japan, but if there is enough demand, Toshiba may have the incentive to introduce the product in other countries.

Not all fibers collected for reuse are suitable to be made into paper. Squak Mountain Stone has created a product from postconsumer recycled paper and industrial waste that can be used for bathroom and kitchen countertops and tiles for backsplashes and floors. The postconsumer material is mixed waste paper, and the post-industrial content is coal fly-ash from a Washington-based coal-fired electrical generation plant and crushed glass (crystalline silica-free).

TREE-FREE PAPER

Tree-free paper is made using fibers from nontree sources. Tree-free paper can be divided into two types. Organic tree-free paper uses material derived from plant sources such as residues from agricultural crops, or plants grown specifically for papermaking such as hemp, bamboo, and kenaf. Nonorganic tree-free paper is usually made of plastic polymers or minerals. Even though tree-free papers have been around for several decades they have yet to capture a significant share of the paper market. It is important to note that some manufacturers consider any paper that uses no virgin fiber to be tree-free even though some products may actually contain a sizable amount of recycled wood fiber. Advocates for the use of alternative papers argue that tree-free paper is beneficial because these products save virgin trees. However, once the full life cycle of individual products are analyzed their environmental benefits are not always as impressive as they first seem. To date, the best options in tree-free papers are those that are made from agricultural waste that would otherwise be thrown away or burned.

Costa Rica Natural Paper Co. makes products both for off the shelf use and for offset and digital printing. Their paper is available in a variety of weights, colors, and textures, depending on what crop waste or excess was used to produce it.

Organic Tree-Free Papers

Tree-free papers can provide an alternative to either recycled or virgin wood derived pulp. Even though some types of tree-free fibers (such as agricultural residues) can be produced with fewer chemicals, less energy, and less water than wood, the development of these materials for widespread consumer use has not yet occurred. In most cases tree-free fiber is more expensive, not available in large quantities, and faces challenges in manufacturing because mills may have to be redesigned or retrofitted to accommodate these new materials in the paper-making process. Agricultural residues (including coffee, banana, wheat, and rice residue) are considered the most preferable material to be used for paper production because these residues would otherwise go to waste.

Kenaf, hemp, and bamboo all grow in a matter of months rather than years and have been touted as wonder materials for paper production. However, the use of annual crops is complex and not advocated even by most environmental groups. Studies comparing the use of annual crops such as kenaf or bamboo to tree plantations do not necessarily support the substitution of these fibers for wood pulp. Annual crops may require more frequent doses of fertilizer and pesticides to produce the same amount of fiber and do not provide the secondary benefits of tree plantations, including wildlife habitats, carbon trapping, and water-quality protection. The use of annual non-tree derived fibers is still in its infancy and will require further investment and development before becomeing a viable alternative to tree pulp.

Materials That Can Produce Organic Tree-Free Paper	Kenaf, hemp, bamboo, sugar cane, cotton (from rags or rolls), agricultural residues (such as coffee, banana, rice, wheat, corn, and rye)

Nonorganic Tree-Free Papers

The future of nonorganic tree-free paper may lie in technological innovation and the development of new materials that are designed for reuse. For example, William McDonough and Michael Braungart's book *Cradle to Cradle* is printed on a synthetic waterproof and tree-free "paper" called Durabook, which is produced by Melcher Media. Synthetic papers are smooth, come in different weights, take four-color process inks, and use no or limited wood or cotton fiber in their production. Unfortunately, while technically recyclable, without special recycling facilities items printed on synthetics will most likely to end up in landfills.

Another pioneering product, TerraSkin, is produced by Chameleon, which is the environmental division of Design and Source Production Inc. TerraSkin is a tree-free paper made from minerals that will eventually degrade back to powdered stone from which it was made.

None of these new applications are perfect, and most are considerably heavier than wood pulp paper. But these products do represent new opportunities for increased choice in environmentally preferable materials. They may one day prove that we really can invent our way out of the paper problem.

Polyart uses a unique combination of paper and plastic to create a high performance product that is extremely durable, water resistant, and accepts either water-based, solvent, or UV inks. Polyart can be used for brochures, hangtags, labels, maps, and packaging.

Botanical note cards made from mango paper, banana paper, and coffee paper. Costa Rica Natural Paper Co. products are made from a mixture of 100 percent unbleached postconsumer recycled fiber. Their products also contain at least 5 percent agricultural by-product.

The paper is made without added chemicals or additives. By developing and marketing tree-less paper, Costa Rica Natural Paper Co. uses and removes 230,000 tons of agro-industrial waste that are dumped yearly in Costa Rica.

FAST TRACK TO THE EXPERTS

For designers who want to specify environmentally responsible print production but don't want to or have the time to do a lot of legwork themselves, print brokers and distributors can be great resources. These experts amass an impressive amount of information from a variety of vendors and can help advise designers about the best choices for the environment, the job, and cost.

Environmental Print Brokers

A print broker works independently as a middleman between print production providers and their customers. A broker may have preferential relationships with the printers that they represent. This often translates into intimate knowledge of a facility's capabilities and potential cost savings for the customer. Because brokers deal exclusively with production, they are usually aware of the newest materials and innovations in the printing industry. Brokers can be fantastic resources for designers who don't have time to learn all the nuances of environmentally friendly print production.

Print Broker Responsibilities	• Provide both client and manufacturing referrals, product samples, explain what services they will provide
	• Understand the print production process and facilities of the printers he/she represents, including third-party certifications
	• Work with a vendor to provide carbon usage calculations for each job and show where vendors obtain the energy to operate their facilities
	• Provide competitive rates for all services, including options and quotes from several different vendors with comparisons of both cost savings and environmental commitment in specified areas
	• Have a working knowledge of the specifications for recycled paper, tree-free paper, process chlorine-free paper and FSC-certified paper
	• Walk a designer through the process of producing a sustainable print solution from start to finish regardless of previous knowledge or production experience

Some print brokers advertise themselves as specializing in green printing, while others simply offer this expertise as one among many services. Generally brokers offer the greatest cost advantages for jobs greater than $10,000. But if a designer is specing something as complicated as eco-friendly printing, brokers can easily make their commissions (which is paid for by the printers they represent) worthwhile for small runs even if the savings to a customer are minimal.

Print brokers are most often located in larger metropolitan areas, but you shouldn't feel limited to working with a broker that is close to home. For example, using a broker can make a lot of sense for designers who live in relatively remote areas but work with clients who are based in nearby cities or even across the country. In this case, working with a printer near the materials manufacturer or in the same area as a client can make a lot of sense. Also, a broker may be able to obtain preferential pricing at a superior printing facility that is near materials manufacturer or in the same area as a client. If the environmental benefits are large enough, they may outweigh the costs and energy used to ship the finished product.

Greg Barber has specialized in environmental printing since 1990, the twentieth anniversary of Earth Day. Barber says in the 1990s fewer than 5 percent of designers knew the definitions of environmental print terms. Today, Barber works with hand-picked printers and offers both digital and offset printing services. He saves clients money, answers questions, is a resource for sustainable printing, and knows which products to recommend for every kind of job and budget. Barber has all sorts of way to save money while being eco-friendly. "I offer co-op printing so I can put several clients together on the same paper and save them all a lot of money," he says. One of the best deals Barber offers clients is 100 percent postconsumer waste papers that are less expensive than some non eco-friendly papers and equal in price to most grades with 30 percent postconsumer waste sheets.

Barber doesn't think cost should be a deterrent if one wants to print sustainably. "Sometimes designers are afraid to recommend environmental printing to their clients because they are afraid the cost will hurt their chances on getting the design jobs. I tell them you need to be speaking with me," he says.

Paper Distributors

Printers usually purchase paper from distributors rather than directly from the mills that produce the product. Distributors therefore work directly with consumers while maintaining close relationships with representatives at paper companies. Large distributors often have specific employees who educate designers about new products and trends in the paper industry. Because distributors are in business to sell paper, but not necessarily a specific brand or type, they have a vested interest in seeing that paper products meet the needs of the design industry.

As an example of a paper distributor, Unisource is the largest privately held paper distributor in the U.S. It sells both fine and industrial printing papers and supplies. Andrew Dembitz, director of specification at the company's Chicago office, acts as an intermediary between designers and the paper companies whose products Unisource represents. "I inform the design market about the latest trends in the world of paper and can act as a consultant on projects to help the designer make the right decision about the grade of paper that they select," Dembitz says.

Unisource's Chicago location was the first division in the company to be FSC-certified, which means that the chain of custody for FSC products remains continuous through Unisource distribution. "The environment is a hot topic," says Dembitz. He has found that "all the mills have a 'green' story," and he underscores the benefit of working with someone who represents a variety of companies. "Relying only on printers for paper information can sometimes be a mistake," he cautions. "Printers may recommend a sheet that is their 'house' stock as opposed to a sheet that was right for the job, and a printer is not going to be aware of all of the possibilities or the latest trends." The benefit to designers of having an intermediary person as a resource is that they're objective and privy to the latest market information.

London-based socially conscious designer and illustrator Chris Haughton's cover for the Spring/Summer 2006 People Tree catalogue. People Tree produces gifts and clothing through groups and projects set up to employ minorities or disabled people in the developing world who are without access to social welfare.

These People Tree handmade paper cards are individually printed in the workshop at Eastern Screen Printers in Saidpur, in northern Bangladesh. The paper itself is made from all waste materials. The fiber wastes come from either pineapple, jute, or pond water hyacinth.

by Blake Coglianese, assistant
professor of graphic design at the
University of North Florida

WASTE NOT, WANT NOT

The role of a designer is undoubtedly a demanding one: You have obligations to your boss, your clients, yourself, and the project at hand. However, a graphic designer's responsibility to the environment is often overlooked and underestimated. Every day, we make decisions on behalf of consumers by specifying papers, inks, and special printing techniques that visually enhance our work, often without realizing the environmental consequences of our decisions. Designers who want to be proactive and minimize the consumption of natural resources can make relatively small changes to benefit both our clients and the environment.

Proof On Screen, Off Paper

Every day in design studios around the world, office printers are going nonstop. For example, the headline size of a brochure is changed from 24-point type to 26-point type, and the designer prints out another paper proof to view the change. Fifteen minutes later, the headline color changes from PMS 648 to PMS 647, and another sheet of paper runs through the printer. While the nuances of design do require a close examination, you can be much more efficient and reduce an enormous amount of paper waste by proofing onscreen as much as possible before you print.

The Environmental Protection Agency (EPA) estimates that waste paper constitutes 90 percent of all office waste by weight, and it ends up in landfills if not recycled. If you really have to print, such as in-house memos and proofs that will not go to a client, it is easy to make a simple change and use both sides of the paper.

Educate the Consumer

Minimizing waste isn't just about the designer; it's about the end-user as well. Though recycling was on a solid and steady rise for about twenty years, recent studies indicated that consumers are not recycling as much as they used to. One study estimates that consumer recycling has fallen by almost 5 percent in recent years. Many experts attribute this apathy to the fact that recycling isn't new or trendy anymore. Others say that recycling has become an inconvenience, even though an EPA study shows that on average it takes just over two minutes a day to separate your recycling from your trash.

In many cases, it is not about being inconvenienced, but rather about being uncertain. Consumers are often unsure of which products can and cannot be recycled. This is especially true in localities without formal recycling programs.

Designers should place a high priority on ensuring that the consumer knows a product is recyclable. In just a small area of real estate on the package or printed piece, you can add the recycling logo or a phrase that signifies the product's recyclability. By indicating that a package design or printed piece uses recycled content or vegetable-based inks, for example, you can inform the consumers that they are making smart choices on behalf of the environment. That makes good marketing sense.

Product is recyclable

Product is made using recycled materials

Consider Size

The size of the paper your project will be printed on typically exceeds the dimensions of your original design. Printers will fit as many pages of your design onto one sheet as is possible. Your objective should be to choose the most appropriate paper size for the project, keeping in mind that the U.S. printing industry uses multiples of the 8½ x 11-inch sheet as a basis for their paper stock sizes. In many cases, your printer will assist you in this process, but knowing beforehand what is available enables you to make informed decisions during the initial sessions when you think about the size and shape of your project.

If you specify an unusual size for your layout, a large amount of the paper will go unused, which wastes resources and money because paper is typically one of the higher costs in the production process. While the unused paper will be trimmed and recycled, simply adjusting the size of your design can allow you to use the paper more efficiently.

If you do have to create a design at a size that leaves a lot of trimmed waste, consider including another project on the print run to use the excess paper space. Or you could work directly with a paper manufacturer to develop a custom paper size specifically for your project. This will insure that you are using the most effective paper size for your needs and will reduce waste.

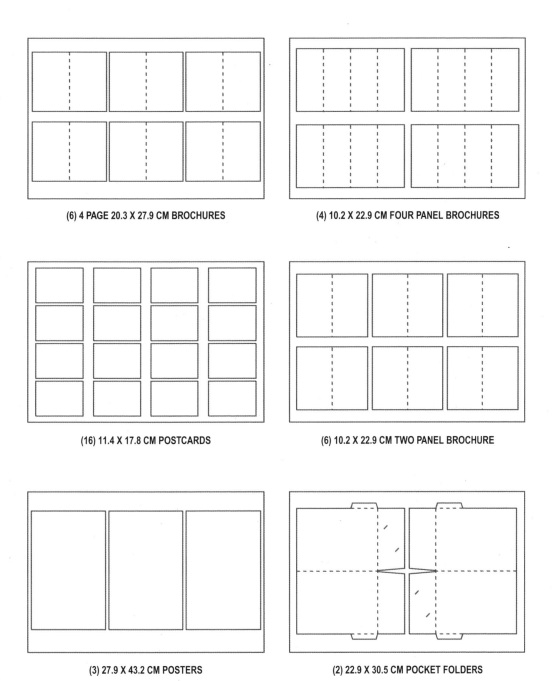

(6) 4 PAGE 20.3 X 27.9 CM BROCHURES

(4) 10.2 X 22.9 CM FOUR PANEL BROCHURES

(16) 11.4 X 17.8 CM POSTCARDS

(6) 10.2 X 22.9 CM TWO PANEL BROCHURE

(3) 27.9 X 43.2 CM POSTERS

(2) 22.9 X 30.5 CM POCKET FOLDERS

Basic U.S. Sheet Sizes: 17 × 11 inches, 23 × 35 inches, 25 × 38 inches, 26 × 40 inches, 28 × 40 inches, 35 × 23 inches

Note: Not all paper stocks come in all of these sizes. Check with your printer before beginning a project.

Curb the Ink Flow

Another way to create a more environmentally friendly piece is to use less ink. Reduce the number of inks required to print your project, or better yet, reduce the amount of ink coverage in your design. Incorporate more white space into your layout, use fewer or smaller photos, vignette the photos, or use screened colors. Unless the success of your design hinges on a specific color, talk to your printer about using the ink already on the press from a previous job. As a result, less ink will become waste and the chemicals used in cleaning the press is reduced.

As you design, think ahead to how your product will be disposed of. Ideally, it will be recycled. As it is being recycled, each page will go through a de-inking process, in which ink is removed from the page. The de-inking process leaves behind a sludge containing ink, dyes, adhesives, staples, and other contaminates that must be disposed of. By anticipating the disposal stage of your product, you are working toward a better understanding of cradle to grave design, and you are limiting the amount of waste that ultimately ends up in a landfill.

Lay Off the Trigger

Today, many businesses rely on a shotgun approach to marketing. Company literature is sent to hundreds or thousands of people in hopes that a few will respond. You can reduce wasted resources by carefully researching and targeting your audience, making sure you are reaching your prime audience with maximum efficiency. Instead of creating a direct mail piece for 10,000 prospective customers, a designer can do some additional research and create a targeted, personalized campaign for 1,000 more likely prospects and a more cost-effective and less paper-intensive job.

While you probably won't be able to incorporate every suggestion into each project you work on, even a few changes in your design process will make a noticeable difference. Your decisions will have a positive effect on the environment, and you might be surprised to learn that some of these tips will save you and your client time and money.

by Michael Hardt, design consultant in Saarbrücken, Germany, former vice president of ICOGRADA, and former chairman of the European Designers Association (BEDA)

PHOTO CREDIT: ZANE LICITE, RIGA LATVIA

SUSTAINABLE PACKAGING

Although packaging in the larger sense is likely as old as mankind, packaging as we know it today has a rather short history. It is only in the past 100 years that we started to use prepackaged goods on a larger scale.

Good packaging has improved peoples' lives. Without contemporary packaging, we would be even less able to feed the growing world population. World hunger is a huge problem, and it mostly occurs in areas of the world where packaging is less developed.

While packaging can solve some problems, it also generates new problems. Creating packaging wastes and destroys valuable resources, energy, and material. Packaging pollutes the world.

Different interest groups make the decisions about packaging. Each of the groups that follow considers itself to be most important, but only sees one aspect of the entire problem:

• Packaging engineers choose the technology and the materials.
• Controllers make decisions about the costs of packaging.
• Marketing and sales people want the packaging to be attractive.

Governments often create contradictory rules and guidelines when it comes to packaging and materials. The European Packaging Directive is one such example—under this directive, industries are forced to reduce the amount of packaging and improve their recycling methods. But at the same time, other directives require additional packaging for hygienic reasons. For example, some small items will be put into big packaging just to accommodate the mandatory information texts prescribed by consumer protection laws.

The Problem with Questions

What kind of packaging answer you get depends on the question you ask. If you ask for low-cost packaging, you will get a low-cost solution. If you ask for an advertising pack, you will receive advertising media. And if you ask for a sustainable solution, you will get a sustainable result.

Up until now, customers did not often ask for sustainable solutions in their package design. I once proposed a design, which was the best possible sustainable solution, but it didn't look eco-friendly. The client insisted on using a material that fulfilled the public's expected cliché of ecology, and the final solution looked ecological, but it was not sustainable at all. It was a lie and a fake.

For example, people often think that a glass bottle is a more eco-friendly and sustainable container for liquids than a coated cardboard box. It's true that glass is made out of silicon, which is just sand, an abundant resource, and glass bottles can be used many times. But glass is heavy and needs a lot of energy to manufacture and transport to stores and then back to be reused or recycled. Before the bottle can be reused it has to be cleaned, again using energy, water, and chemicals. Plus, the glass used in packaging lasts forever, while the contents inside usually has an expiration date of less than two months.

On the other hand, the coated cardboard packaging is usually used once and then thrown in the bin. But when you consider all aspects of the use and reuse of each material, the cardboard is a little better than glass. What we really need is a better recycling system for coated cardboard.

Packaging is a complex system, and it isn't limited to the container on the shelf of a supermarket. Before the product appears on a shelf, masses of plastic foils are used to wrap the pallets to protect the cardboard shipment boxes against moisture during transport and storage. Plastic bags are used to transport products home from the store, and plastic garbage bags hold all the disposed products, which then end up in a landfill. In packaging, one has to think about reduction, reuse, and/or recycling.

Better Questions Equal Better Answers

The question should not be, "Can we do better?" but "How can we make things a little less bad?" Sometimes the perfect solution for a small problem can create big problems somewhere else. It is a bad deal when you have to invest $100 to save $10.

There is a difference between eco-friendly and sustainable. The eco-philosophy of the 1970s tried and still tries to save the world completely. No compromise. It is not less whale killing; it is no whale killing. It is not less petrol consumption; it is no petrol consumption. It is not less packaging; it is no packaging. On the other hand, sustainability is a philosophy of compromise. When we damage the world and waste energy, it's harmful. Can we damage less and waste less? Can we do less harm?

Packaging for the Future

For many years, I have taught courses about packaging design at several design colleges in Europe. In the past I used to ask the students to go out to a shop and pick out the worst packaging, describe why it is bad, get information about the reasons, and maybe talk to the producer and develop a better solution. Most of the designs proposed by the students improved the look and the branding, and maybe the handling.

However in the past few years, I began to ask a different question: What will packaging look like twenty years from now, after the death of supermarkets due to the e-buying revolution, in the past-petrol-age, and in the middle of the climate collapse?

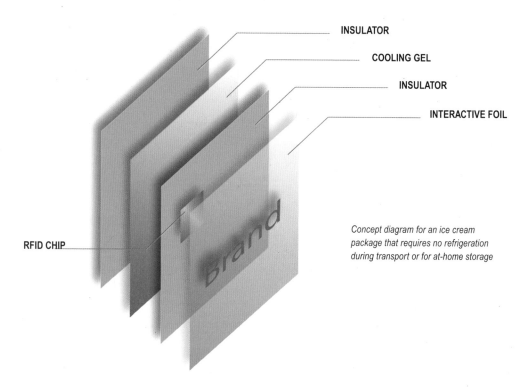

INSULATOR

COOLING GEL

INSULATOR

INTERACTIVE FOIL

RFID CHIP

Concept diagram for an ice cream package that requires no refrigeration during transport or for at-home storage

Now I ask students to design from the future back to the present, and not from today until tomorrow. Ask another question and you will get another answer. It is amazing to see the change in the attitude of design students being faced with a different question.

For example, "Why do we have to cool production facilities when we produce ice cream? What if there were packaging made out of self-cooling material?" When asked these questions, students from the National College of Arts and Design in Dublin, Ireland, started to research if there could be such a material.

Then we asked, "Could this material provide a communicating surface, giving information about the temperature, the expiration date? Could it possibly be interactive, and could this material be reused?" They found answers to their questions.

The student's design solution was a briefing for a new material. Using this material, it would no longer be necessary to cool production facilities, trucks, storage, and shelves, or to put the ice cream box in the fridge. The savings on energy will be much higher than the additional costs for an intelligent packaging. And of course it is not only a solution for ice cream. This material may not exist yet, but it is technically possible.

Another group of students explored the question of packaging ownership. In a number of systems in the past, the consumer did not automatically become the owner of the packaging. For example, the milkman picked up the cleaned empty milk bottle and replaced it with a full bottle. Today, however, most consumers own the packaging after a product is purchased.

Process Precedes Product

Sustainable packaging design is the design of a process rather than the design of a product. The final graphics on the packaging are just decoration, not design.

In nature one can find many genius packaging concepts. Bionics, a new science between biology and technology, can be a resource to help solve packaging problems. Students at the University of Lapland in Rovaniemi, Finland, proposed to breed and tame intelligent microbes to teach them how to shape packaging. After the expiration date of the packed goods, the microbes would recycle the pack content themselves and it become humus (soil). Ashes to ashes, earth to earth. It sounds like science fiction, but you never know. It is often the tiny idea that makes a big difference.

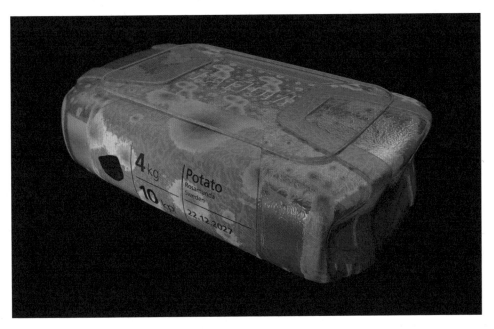

Inspired by the idea that packaging should not last longer than the material in it, students from the University of Lapland designed this package for potatoes that would begin to decompose after the expiration date of the vegetables. This virtual 3-D rendering of the potato pack shows what a package made up of tamed microbes might look like. 3-D rendering by Anssi Ahonen, student in the town of Rovaniemi, Finland.

One group of students from the National Academy of the Arts in Bergen, Norway, wanted to design a new cracker pretzels package, which is a traditional product in Norway. Cracker pretzels arrive in the shop packaged in poorly branded plastic bags. Most of the pretzels crumbled because the packaging was inappropriate for its purpose.

The students' first sketches showed beautiful graphics on a sturdy box. The producer kindly permitted the students to have a look at the production and packaging chain. He questioned why they wanted to redesign the package. They replied, "To be more consumer friendly and sell more pretzels." The producer said, "The problem is not the demand. The problem is the storage space and the transportation capacities."

So the students researched storage and transportation. Looking at the big shipment boxes, they noticed that due to incorrect measurements, 25 percent of space inside the boxes and on the pallets was empty. This meant that 25 percent of the transportation space was also wasted, along with wasted fuel due to extra trips to transport the pretzels.

This example shows how easy it can be to save energy and resources and start to think sustainably. Design the process, don't decorate a product.

Cracker pretzels (called Vannkringler) in their original packaging.

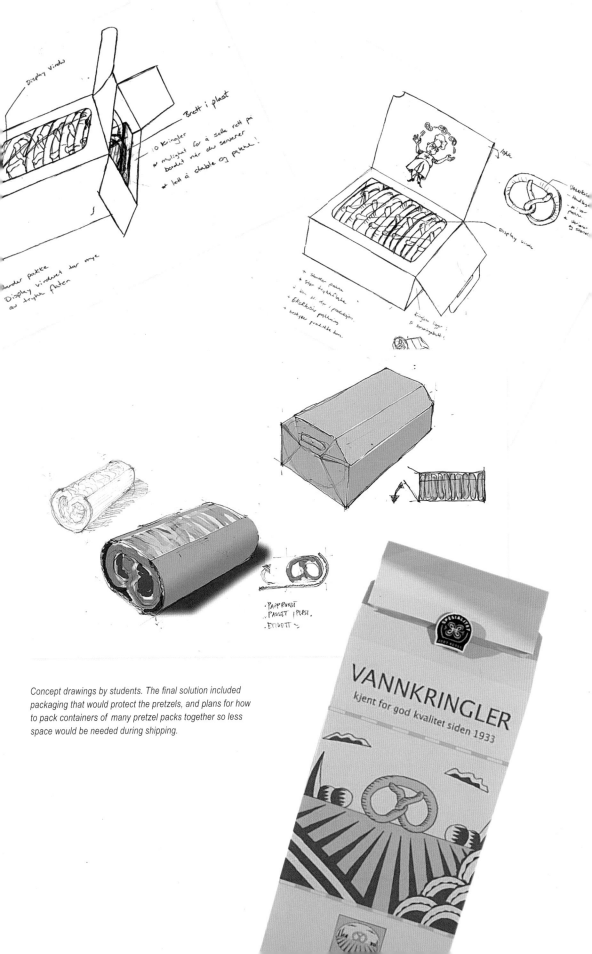

Concept drawings by students. The final solution included packaging that would protect the pretzels, and plans for how to pack containers of many pretzel packs together so less space would be needed during shipping.

Students Jan Erik Kristoffersen, Tomas Jøssang, Ove Dahl, and Bård-Henning Kvinen working on designs for pretzels packaging

Let's Do Things a Little Less Bad

The more one gets into the field of sustainability, the more it is possible to see the chances to increase profit and make money by making things better. I am confident that sustainability will be tomorrow's fastest growing market.

"It's not creative unless it sells," was a famous quote we adhered to back when I studied design. Package design was the face of a product on the shelf in the supermarket. However, packaging design in the future will be a complex balance between economy and ecology, between user and producer, between profit and benefit, and between promise and expectation.

After seeing the results from the next generation of designers, I am very confident that they will make things better than we did, just by asking different questions.

PART TWO	# Putting It to Practice

CHAPTER 4:

Living and Working Sustainably

The designers and companies featured in this chapter are passionate about environmental and social causes but are not united by style, media, or even a single ideology. There is no one right way to work sustainably. It depends on local conditions, on the resources available, and on the specifications for a particular job. Projects produced under the headings *green*, *sustainable*, or *eco-friendly* don't have to look different from other any design work. Increasingly, it is only the use of environmental labeling that allows a viewer to tell whether some thing has been produced using preferable production practices and with social consciousness in mind. In this chapter you will find production specifics, examples of how to frame problems using sustainable thinking, and case studies of design work that includes store displays, websites, and print materials. These designers are eager to share information and want to make adopting sustainable practices easier for others than it was for them.

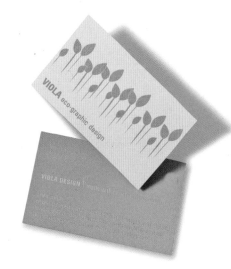

Viola Eco-Graphic Design's business cards, like all of their promotions materials, are friendly and approachable. The design is a visual representation of the company's commitment to make work that is inspired by nature.

VIOLA ECO-GRAPHIC DESIGN

Based in Melbourne, Australia, Viola Eco-Graphic Design is devoted to best practices in ecologically sustainable design. With projects that draw on a range of services, including creative print-based design solutions, social marketing, designing for sustainability, strategic facilitation, and fundraising marketing, Viola demonstrates that visually sophisticated graphic design doesn't have to "cost the earth." Viola founder, Anna Carlile, and her team have developed a diverse portfolio of arresting designs and successful campaigns that integrate ecologically-inspired creativity with environmentally-sensitive production practices. Many of Viola's clients share a passion for positive social change and respect for the environment.

There is a strong "values fit" with organizations that have an environmental, cultural, or community focus. However, Viola designers are also specialized in a number of business sectors and are often asked to share practical ways of adopting sustainable practices with mainstream clients. Carlile emphasizes that when engaging in sustainable design, designers are no longer limited to making work that is any different visually or has a "grass roots" look. "If you look at an ecologically-produced piece, it will often look like every other job," Carlile says. "It was the choices made in the early stages—such as stock and printer selection—that make the piece sustainable."

In addition to working for nonprofits and community organizations, Viola works with businesses that have an interest in commissioning design with minimal environmental impact. For Hazeldene Yarra Valley resort and spa, for example, Viola was asked to design the identity package and a promotional brochure.

Carlile believes sustainability has reached a tipping point in the public's consciousness. As a result, her business has grown rapidly with the help of an increasing number of organizations who have committed to reducing their environmental impact and adopted triple-bottom line economics. (see glossary page 186) "There is enormous opportunity for graphic designers to capture this market by working with governments and companies that have made the environment a primary concern," Carlile says.

It is Carlile's opinion that in the very near future sustainable thinking and a working knowledge of responsible production will be an absolute must for designers. She is encouraging to both professionals and students who want to make the environment or social causes a cornerstone of their practice. "When you act from a place where your heart is and where your values are and you integrate this in a knowledgeable way into your profession, you can then work with like-minded organizations and will have a huge chance of being successful," Carlile says.

To minimize the use of materials, ECO-Buy's 2005/2006 annual report was designed as a downloadable PDF with a summary of the key components printed as a small brochure to be handed out at the launch. The original piece was done as a five-panel concertina fold so it used the full printable area on press (set two up on an oversize sheet). When folded, the brochure fit neatly into a DL envelope for mail-outs.

Melbourne University

Every year Melbourne University produces more than $9 million of printed material. Like many environmentally conscious organizations, the university wanted to explore new ways of meeting their communication needs while also being sensitive to the environment. With this challenge in mind, Viola was asked to develop an internal environmental management manual, with the goal of helping the university adopt new practices that would reduce the environmental impact of its publications.

The result was a comprehensive guide that showcased the potential of eco-design as an environmental discipline. The standard twenty-four page printed brochure was considered but then quickly dismissed, both because of the waste that would be generated and because once printed the information would become dated. Due to the changing nature of the content, a website was approved as the most appropriate communications medium. To promote the use of the website by the university's publication departments, Viola created an innovative, freestanding desktop piece, which required no binding and was both eye-catching and retainable. The printing was sponsored by a cleangreenprint.com initiative and was QIS014001 compliant. The production used low-toxic inks and Envirocare paper that was composed of 65 percent postconsumer and 35 percent preconsumer recycled material and produced by a mill with EMAS (Eco-Management and Audit Scheme) accreditation.

In addition to including pertinent information about how to reduce waste and specify eco-friendly materials, this guide gave statistics about which materials and printing facilities had been used in its production. Viola, repurposed much of the information used for the Melbourne University's print guide and made similar tabletop guides available to the public.

EcoRecycle Victoria

The organizations EcoRecycle Victoria, Centre for Design, and The Design Institute Australia formed a partnership to inspire industrial designers to embrace eco-design. Viola was brought in to create a communication piece using eco-design principles to demonstrate that eco-design could have contemporary imagery and great visual style.

After studying the problem and brainstorming various solutions, Viola designers decided to create a brochure that opened up into a poster. The dual uses of this piece would maximize impact by combining content and efficiently using the design space. With eco-design principles in mind, the initial A2 page format was rejected in favor of the A3. This reduced the resources used by half and delivered significant cost savings while maintaining creative impact.

The brochure outlined the core steps required in Design for Environment and used a visual aesthetic that would be easily understood by product designers. Focus testing ensured that the design would resonate with the targeted audience. Information sheets using the same content were also developed in PDF format for easy distribution. By creating a PDF version of a printed piece one can save on unnecessary printing costs and minimize waste when it is difficult to ascertain quantities needed. Having both printed and digital versions of the same content allowed end users two entry points to the same data.

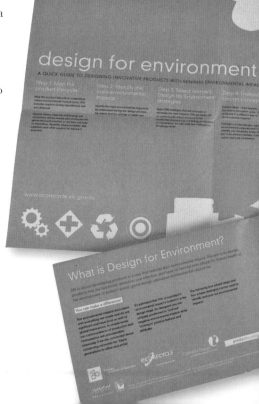

The Design for Environment brochure/ poster gave basic strategies for minimizing a product's impact on the environment and promoted the Eco-Recycle Victoria website as a resource for product designers to obtain further information.

The final design product from Viola is an expression of total beauty—a combination of our inspired creativity and our commitment to protect the natural environment.

ANNA CARLILE – founder of Viola

International Women's Development Agency

The International Women's Development Agency (IWDA) hired Viola to design something special for its 2005–2006 annual report. Inspired by efficiency and collaborative thinking, Carlile and her team decided to combine the traditional annual report with a fully functioning calendar. Merging the two would allow the annual report content to take on a second life as a beautiful gift to thank committed supporters. Using a collection of striking photographs, which were especially chosen to reflect the work and values of IWDA, this dual communication piece paired financial statements and the president's report with inspiring stories of IWDA initiatives and a calendar for each month in the upcoming year.

IWDA's firm commitment to reducing the environmental impact from their print publications allowed the organization to enter into a sponsorship partnership with cleangreenprint.com, K.W. Doggetts, and Viola. As a result, the annual report/calendar was printed by an ISO14001 compliant printer with an environmental management system, using nontoxic inks and sealing varnishes, on 100 percent recycled papers.

Carlile is committed to helping clients get the most out of production materials and her services. "The duality of this communication piece ensured it would have greater retainability and usage as a marketing tool," Carlile says. "In doing so, the environmental cost was cleverly minimized."

Every year Viola designs the International Women's Development Agency's (IWDA) annual report using the creative format of a calendar/report combination. Viewers can easily navigate through the annual report information, and they are given a nice take away piece in the calendar.

Accessible Information

Carlile, working through Viola, has made a unique commitment to work toward minimizing the impact of the design industry on the environment. She recently earned a master's of the environment degree from the University of Melbourne. Carlile is as passionate about sharing what she has learned about responsible production and sustainable business as she is about making great design. "For us, leading the way with sustainable design practices isn't enough," she says. "We also educate and inspire others to change their ways through our eco-design consulting and workshops."

The community activism arm of Viola, which is called Design by Nature, is a collaborative effort with the Centre for Design and Eco-Design Foundation. Design by Nature is an extensive online resource forum for environmentally sustainable graphic design in Australia. The website targets key areas that need consideration when creating environmentally-sensitive design and includes useful information such as paper and printing guides and examples of great sustainable design. www.designbynature.org

PLAZM DESIGN

Plazm magazine was founded in 1991 as a creative resource for artists. Four years later, the company launched Plazm Design, a multidisciplinary studio dedicated to serving both commercial clients and social causes. Today, Plazm Design is committed to investing in their local community by fostering artistic development, creating and sponsoring public events, and initiating and distributing alternative media. Plazm Design's model for social involvement is an integral part of company policy. "Donating time that could otherwise be used for billable hours to cause-related projects adds to the sustainability of the community in which we live and is a part of Plazm's core mission," says Joshua Berger, creative director and managing partner of Plazm Design. "We believe design has the power to change the world."

For Nike's Considered line of footwear products, Plazm Design designers explored environmentally responsible materials while still making a great looking promotions piece.

The first pages of the spiral-bound media kit brochure are devoted to product specifications and important information about the product line.

Nike Considered BB High

Nike Considered BB Low
Men's

Nike Considered BB Low
Men's

CONSIDER DESIGN

CONSIDERED PRODUCT CONSTRUCTION IS ABOUT DOING MORE WITH LESS.

CLASSIC B-BALL

X-STITCH

NIKE

EMBOSS OR LASER SWOOSH

FREE BOTTOM IN PHYLITE.

SEAM TURNED OUT FOR SUPPORT & COMFORT (ONE LAYER BODY-SHAPE)

VENT PEEK IN VAMP + TONGUE

THIN BINDING FOR STRENGTH

The focus is on using less materials and harmful chemicals while maintaining performance.

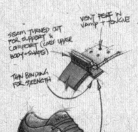

PHYLITE MIDSOLE/OUT-SOLE = LIGHT + DURABLE + FLEXIBLE

MINIMAL MATERYL

Nike Considered

For the Asia/Pacific arm of retail giant Nike, Plazm Design was asked to create a media kit for a new series of footwear. The Considered product line is Nike's collection of environmentally-conscious footwear. The shoes are made with vegitan leather, hemp laces and stitching, no adhesives, recycled rubber soles, and other eco-friendly features. The challenge, and Plazm Design's designers' goal for the project, was to create a kit that would be true to the ideals of the product while still presenting an elegant and convincing media package.

Plazm designers initiated a solution that used a leather billfold as the package anchor and housing for the kit assets. The billfold was durable and reusable, and it was made from the same vegitan leather as the shoes and stitched with hemp thread. No adhesives were used, and the logo was stamped blind on the cover with no ink or foils.

The text content of the kit was printed on the first few pages of a reporter's standard size spiral notepad. The back pages were left mostly blank for notetaking, but they included a series of "Considered" messages at the bottom of each sheet. The book itself was printed with soy-based inks on 100 percent postconsumer recycled paper. "The only thing we couldn't source using recycled material was the CD, which was a client requirement," Berger says.

Plazm Design's workload is split evenly between cause-related work and corporate clients. Berger suggests partnerships enable designers to affect real change. He believes that simple steps—such as specifying recycled paper—can make a difference, but that designers also have the opportunity to engage in open discussions with clients about social responsibility and even connect corporations with community nonprofits.

Berger thinks the best part about the Nike Considered project was that it was an example of a corporate assignment with high social values that was client initiated. He concludes, "The piece was successful in that it met both the client's communication goals and their goals to use only sustainable materials."

The last pages of the Considered product brochure were designed as a notepad so that users would be motivated to give the piece a longer life by continuing to use it.

CONSIDER CONSEQUENCES

CONSIDER EFFORT

CONSIDER DESIGN

GUERRINI ISLAND

Argentinean graphic designer Sebastian Guerrini has made sustainability one of the main focuses of the work produced by his studio GuerriniIsland. Because Guerrini lives and works in a place where environmental issues are not always a primary concern for the local government, and eco-friendly production can be cost prohibitive, Guerrini targets social and political issues as well as environmentally responsible production. He believes that social activism and best practice production are equally important components of working toward a sustainable future. "I accept that I must compromise on environmental issues and stress how I can contribute my activity toward philosophical and political changes in our culture," he says.

Ideology and Design

Guerrini suggests that designers should begin by questioning the society in which they exist. This opinion was informed by having experienced the conditions brought on by Argentina's economic crisis in 2001. "We should ask why we have a society that attacks the environment and what are the social conditions of the people who have to live in that environment," Guerrini says. "Designers always have the chance to reduce pollution by selecting certain paper and ink and choosing the right materials, but if we are not concerned about our social responsibilities as communicators then we are not doing all that we should."

Visual identity for La Utopia, a company specializing in eco-tourism and organic production of cereal, oleaginous, and meat, in 2005

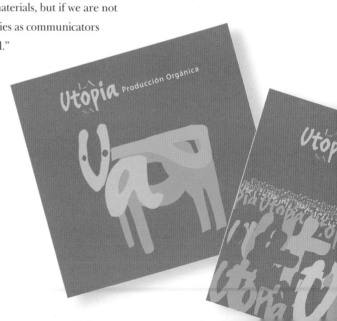

Visual identity for all the programs for recycling and reforestation programs for the Chascomús City Council

When It's Pixels not Paper

A large portion of Guerrini's work deals with image strategy and branding for international clients. While he may have some control over how a corporate identity manual is produced, Guerrini is rarely in a position to specify production standards for all of a company's assets, especially when a client is based in a different country. In such cases, Guerrini's job may be finished when he sends final design files to the client. Guerrini is realistic about the amount of impact a designer can have in such situations, and says, "This kind of professional relationship sometimes limits the influence that one can have about costs and qualities of materials, because most of the time production is handled by local agencies or studios. In such cases, production might be handled by others."

Guerrini created the identity package and designed and illustrated a book on the environment for Nuevo Ambiente, Buenos Aires.

Challenging Circumstances

Because Guerrini is unable to control all aspects of the production process for one sector of his business, he pays special attention to the social and environmental ramifications of his work when he has clients that are closer to home. "With local clients, I work mainly with Grafikar, a printing office that recirculates and processes wastes, and therefore avoids water and soil contamination," Guerrini says. Grafikar was one of the first presses in Argentina to offer environmentally responsible printing services. They spec materials from Europe that comply with international standards that include chlorine free and 50 percent postconsumer waste content for paper and inks that contain fewer heavy metals and solvents. The company shares Guerrini's belief that ultimately sustainability means balancing social and environmental considerations. Beyond the environmental benefits, Grafikar is also concerned with protecting its employees from the harmful toxins that can be part of the printing process.

In Argentina, the cost of using papers with high postconsumer waste content is higher than it is in the United States or Europe. "Totally recycled paper can be as much as seven times more expensive than paper with no PCW content," says Guerrini. "Cheaper sheets are available on the market, but they are poor quality. Here, only cardboard uses almost fully recycled content." It isn't surprising that Guerrini has found that choosing eco-friendly production materials can be cost prohibitive even for clients who would prefer such methods be used on their jobs.

Guerrini's work as both a designer and advisor to environmental projects is extensive. He was a consultant for a recycling program in the city of Buenos Aires, and he has also worked for smaller towns—La Plata, Bahía Blanca, and Chascomús—on similar projects. He has partnered with environmental consultancies in England, and he is currently working with the environmental organization Societat Orgànica in Barcelona, Spain.

Ecomaterials

For the Ecomaterials exhibition and accompanying publication, Guerrini worked with Societat Orgànica, an organization of sustainably-minded architects who were asked to develop an exhibition for a concrete fair in Oporto, Portugal. The goals of the project were to provide answers to the philosophical questions associated with production and recycling in the construction industry and also to encourage people to try to find new technological solutions for making materials that are less damaging to the environment. Of the assignment, Guerrini says, "We wondered whether it would be possible to show a concept of ecomaterials that would be capable of influencing the construction market as a whole."

For the Ecomaterials logo, Guerrini combined visual elements from the internationally recognized symbol for recycling with a simplified rendition of an Ouroboros, which is an ancient Greek symbol of a serpent or dragon swallowing its own tail. Guerrini's goal was to visually reproduce the circular sensibility of use and reuse.

Ecomaterials identity

While working on the Ecomaterials project, Guerrini consciously avoided using a visual aesthetic that would be familiar to architects. "You have to break with what people expect to find and challenge their expectations," he says. "By capturing some part of what is familiar in a different context or environment, you think more about what is around you."

For Guerrini, simplicity is paramount. He believes designers often try to find solutions that are more complicated than they need to be. "We waste time and resources and complicate our own reality," he says. "Something that is very simple can more appropriately reflect one's own environment and life."

Guerrini collected interesting-looking refuse at his local recycling station. By putting several objects together or creating entire installations, he produced more than fifty vignettes to draw a viewer's attention to the exhibition content. In the studio, with the help of a photographer, he documented the compositions and the resulting images were used for posters, exhibit panels, and exhibit publications. Guerrini used best production practices when producing the deliverables for ecomaterials. He believes he will have more impact designing content so an audience begins to care about the environment and social issues than he will ever have by simply specing recycled paper and vegetable-based inks.

The Ecomaterials exhibit used posters, designed by Guerrini, to educate professionals from the construction industry about new materials, emerging technology, and different ways of using resources that could be less harmful to the environment. The exhibition and accompanying publication was so well received that Guerrini and his partners at Societat Orgànica were asked to redo and expand the exhibit for a similar fair in London.

The Ecomaterials book used much of the same visual content as the posters and exhibit panels, but it included additional text and diagrams that detailed materials and processes. Guerrini purposely juxtaposed his playful sculptures and installations with the technical information about construction materials and philosophical rational for minimizing impact on the environment.

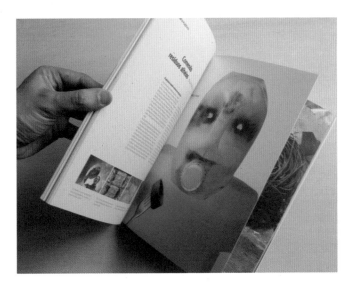

NAU

A growing number of businesses have been founded on sustainable principles. This allows them to build on core concepts such as environmental responsibility and social conscience from the beginning. The high-performance clothing company, Nau, is one of these. Based in Portland, Oregon, Nau was born with sustainability as part of its mission. The Nau website describes the company with the simple statement: "We are a small group of people committed to the power of business as a force for change. Defined by what we love and how we work and play, we are looking to do more than make clothes; we're seeking to redefine what it means to be successful."

Deserving to Exist

Nau founders began by asking if the world really needed another clothing company and wondered whether it would be ethical to add additional products to a world "overflowing with consumer goods." Arriving at the answer that they deserved to exist only if their products and practices would contribute to positive and substantive change, Nau began selling clothing made from high-performance sustainable materials in 2007.

Nau is lean and has the maneuverability to bend the brand to the company's social and environmental ethics. Its talented in-house designers are just as concerned about the sustainable production of building materials, clothing tags, and packaging as they are about growing a successful business. Nau graphic designer Karen Wolf isn't even tempted to use nonsustainable production practices anymore. "Once it's in your blood you can't go back," she says. "I can't even think about going back to using metallic inks!"

Exterior view of a Nau

A Sustainable Retail Environment

Nau's creative director Hal Arneson believes that, when trying to work sustainably, being a start-up has advantages. "There are no legacy problems to deal with," he says. "We brought a lot of experience with us from Patagonia, which was known primarily as a catalog company." At Patagonia, Arneson and his team struggled with the high environmental impact that comes with catalogs and decided that Nau should go another route. "We wondered, do we really want to get into the paper business when we have the luxury of starting from scratch?" Arneson says. Ultimately, Nau became a brand that was much more comfortable existing online and in a few retail locations called Webfronts.

Nau Webfronts blend the traditional store experience with online shopping. Customers are encouraged to try on clothing in the store, but they are invited to make purchases at kiosks that will send merchandise directly from the warehouse to their home. The design strategy for Webfronts focuses on a unique prefabricated concept that provides a consistent and efficient build-out process. "First of all, we look for opportunities to repurpose or salvage existing elements from new locations," says Scott Fedje, Nau's Webfront creative director says.

Unconcerned that customers might notice the leftovers from a location's previous tenants, Fedje believes that, "True sustainable design considers what can be left standing at the starting point. Since the customer experience envelope is premanufactured, existing floors, walls, and ceilings can potentially be reused."

Nau Webfront lighting uses ceramic halide fixtures with fluorescent accents. Scott Fedje, Nau's Webfront creative director, says, "Without sacrificing quality of light, Nau's power efficiencies surpass the strictest energy conservation codes."

Event invitations use handmade paper made with recycled cotton and poppy seeds. They are printed with soy-based ink on a letterpress and can be safely returned to the Earth. "The idea behind this piece is to 'seed' positive change in our community," says Ian Yolles, vice president of marketing. "Having our friends (and chosen influencers) hand out invitations to join us in dialogue helps us connect and grow in our community."

nau

POSITIVE CHANGE BEGINS AT HOME,
A CONVERSATION WITH DEE WILLIAMS

When Dee Williams decided to change her life, she started at home, redefining the very idea of what "home" means and how it affects our relationships.

Come listen to Dee's story, join in the dialog, and become part of the collective.

SEE(D) CHANGE

We're committed to building and supporting healthy communities. These events are conducted in that spirit, in an effort to connect people with the places they live and work, and to bring a diverse group of individuals together in order to incite dialog, inspire action and plant seeds of positive change.

YOUR HOSTS:
NAU®
nau.com
WESTERN STATES CENTER
westernstatescenter.org
1000 FRIENDS OF OREGON
friends.org

WEDNESDAY
APRIL 4, 2007
7PM

PORT VILLAGE
BRIDGEPORT ROAD
TIGARD OR, 97224

SPACE IS LIMITED
RSVP REQUIRED TO:
HOME@NAU.COM

LIGHT FOOD • DRINK

Nau, 1000 Friends of Oregon & Western States Center warmly invite you and a guest to an evening of thoughtful dialog and interaction at the newly opened Nau store.

POSITIVE CHANGE BEGINS AT HOME
A CONVERSATION WITH DEE WILLIAMS

SEE(D) CHANGE
7PM WEDNESDAY APRIL 4, 2007

nau

INSTRUCTIONS FOR RE-USING YOUR INVITATION
SOAK PAPER IN WATER FOR A FEW HOURS. PLACE IN A POT OF SOIL OR GARDEN AND COVER LIGHTLY. KEEP OUT OF DIRECT SUNLIGHT. WATER TWICE A DAY TO KEEP MOIST. OUT OF RESPECT FOR NATIVE SPECIES AND FRAGILE AREAS, PLEASE PLANT THESE ONLY IN DOMESTIC GARDENS. ENJOY YOUR POPPIES.

HANDCRAFTED PAPER MADE FROM RECYCLED COTTON
LETTERPRESSED USING SOY BASED INKS

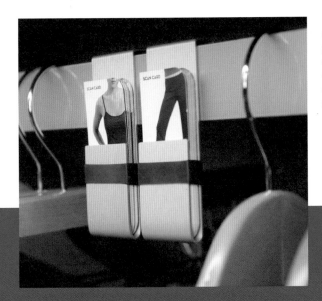

Each item comes with a corresponding product card, which customers can scan at in-store kiosks to display information about materials, production, and social initiatives associated with the design of a particular product.

Kiosks allow customers to have self-service retail experiences. Incentives are given for people willing to wait for an item to be shipped for home delivery rather than immediately taking it out of the store.

Interior environments are created using back
and side panels that are cut and then assembled
in 4 × 10-inch fixture modules. These form the
backbone of the retail environment and are the
primary means of product presentation.

Nau wanted the Lookbook to be visually simple. It was designed using straight backer board and stamping with linen stitching.

The company's commitment to environmentally-responsible design continues with the materials that make up store interiors. "The installed environment is primarily fabricated with Aries, a formaldehyde-free, recycled MDF (medium density fiberboard)," Fedje says. Prior to construction, diagrams of the different shaped pieces are mapped out to minimize waste. The secondary materials used in construction are reclaimed wood, mostly from locally demolished buildings, recycled rubber flooring, 98 percent recycled aluminum, recycled leather fitting room curtains, and FSC-certified alder hangers. Even the mannequins are produced from recyclable resin in a fume-free environment.

Uniting all Nau's collateral pieces is the underlying belief that design must serve a purpose and should be informed by the company's core values of performance, beauty, and sustainability. The limited-edition Fall 2007 Nau Lookbook was produced with 100 percent recycled paper (50 percent was postconsumer) and was printed digitally to minimize waste. "This piece is a statement about our product," Arneson explains. "We wanted to portray a fine-crafted feel without looking too homemade."

Similarly, clothing hangtags are made from 100 percent recycled paper and printed with soy-based inks. The hangtags are key components of the company's efficient distribution system. Each item of clothing starts at the Nau distribution center and needs a bar code so that the piece can be scanned directly, avoiding the need for extra stickers on all of the packages.

Nau is defined by duality. The company exists both online and in the retail environment. It makes products that blend the industrial with the organic, and it refuses to compromise integrity for profitability. By keeping values ahead of the bottom line, Nau continues to redefine what it means to be a retail brand, while providing enduring high-performance clothing for customers that share the company's values.

MONTEREY BAY AQUARIUM

Sustainability dovetails easily with Monterey Bay Aquarium's core
mission of conservation and education. Sustainability is also a consideration
for each part of the promotional material—exhibit design and advertising that's produced
by the aquarium's small, in-house design department. Many of the outreach programs,
conservation initiatives, and member communications are driven by the Aquarium's
commitment to the long-term sustainability of ocean resources. Every piece of aquarium
collateral is conceived and produced to be environmentally and socially conscious.

The Seafood Watch Program

The Seafood Watch program was developed by the Monterey Bay Aquarium to raise
consumer awareness about the importance of purchasing seafood from sustainable sources.
The program includes palm-sized folding purchasing guides and action cards that showcase
different species of threatened ocean life. Goals for the program included attracting new
audiences, presenting a positive choice for consumers, and keeping costs down.

*Action cards combine facts on how the
depletion of ocean species is related to
human consumption with a colorful image of
a fish or crustacean. For example, 100 million
sharks are killed each year for their fins.*

Design director Jim Ales believes that smart effective communications—coupled with disciplined design—is critical to any sustainable program's success. "Our goal was to redefine what an environmental brand could achieve," Ales says. "Our focus was to attract new audiences, presenting a positive choice for consumers."

The design strategy used modern branding models and direct and clear messaging that was delivered in an accessible, consistent visual tone. The designers commissioned life science illustrations to be the foundation for the program. Ales' decision to use illustration rather than photography was intentional. "The highly accurate illustrations foster trust and nurture an emotional connection between people and animals."

Information architecture was developed to be easy to follow and was presented in several languages. The text was typeset in Interstate, which is a highly readable and clean sans serif font. White-coated recycled stock was used for printing and represented an intentional departure from the typical sustainable color palette of browns and greens. Four-color process plus aqueous (water-based) coating further enhanced the styling and aesthetic program. Thirty-six cards were printed on a sheet, using four-color process printing on a six-color press, and in-line aqueous to minimize waste and allow for a single pass on press. Instead of using shrink-wrap, packs of 250 were packaged using paper banding. Both the paper stock and printing process were FSC certified. Approximately fourteen million pocket guides are printed annually with a cost per unit of just under three cents.

Best practice production decisions combined with the program's efficient messaging strategy have proved highly successful. What began as a local consumer awareness campaign has, in the past five years, grown to include a family of seven regional pocket guides that are distributed by sixty-seven partnerships across the United States. The guides are being adopted by a growing list of Seafood Watch partnerships. In 2007, there were 80 partners, including Wal-Mart, Whole Foods, and the Compass Group, the largest catering company in the western hemisphere.

Shorelines *magazine*

Shorelines magazine is delivered three times a year to the aquarium's 75,000 members. It informs aquarium supporters about current events and programs and is designed to be a visual reminder of why members and donors choose to support the aquarium. This sixteen-page magazine is oversized, colorful, and inspiring. To reinforce the aquarium's grand visual experience, beautiful photos and graphics are the cornerstone of the design, accounting for approximately 70 percent of the space.

The page size is 9⅞ x 13⅞-inches, which prints sixteen pages on a single sheet size of 28 x 41-inches without paper waste. The magazine prints 6/6 on a six-color press, one pass per side. The aquarium buys a one-year supply of postconsumer water recycled stock, which gives them an advantage in purchasing power, as well as manufacturing specifics. Paper and printing are both FSC certified.

Each issue, including paper, printing, and postage, costs approximately $1.08, which is less than 1 percent of a single membership. Shorelines magazine is a key component to keeping members connected to the aquarium, which boasts a membership retention rate of 65 percent, one of the highest in the nonprofit sector.

Educational brochures use colorful illustrations of ocean life and are designed to conform to the brand style.

The oversized format of Shorelines magazine helps the piece announce itself in the mailbox and looks impressive on a coffee table.

MONTEREY BAY AQUARIUM · Member MAGAZINE FALL 05

SHORE LINES

3	4	6	12	14
Director's Note	Ocean Policy	Ocean's Edge Whale Wharf	Member Activities	Program Adventures

A larger bat ray pool in our new *Ocean's Edge* galleries offers underwater views.

Inside Stories

Look for some new babies on display in the holdfast exhibit in the Kelp Lab — a wolf-eel (they start life orange), a garibaldi, sheepheads (orange with a white stripe along the side) and several blacksmiths and opaleyes.

We put a small smack of very young northern sea nettles on exhibit in the "tank of the month" in Jellies: Living Art. Though the bells of the jellies were less than two inches in diameter, their tentacles were about a foot long. It makes a dramatic display.

We introduced a subadult giant sea bass into the three-paneled exhibit in the Kelp Gallery after it was donated to us by Cabrillo Marine Aquarium. It's our third individual of this protected California species; we're allowed to keep up to five at one time.

Giant sea bass Stereolepis gigas

Swell shark Cephaloscyllium ventriosum

We tagged and released our white shark on March 31, after a record 198 days here. Thirty days later, her tag popped free and we learned she traveled more than 100 miles offshore, 800 feet deep and 200 miles south of Monterey Bay. She enthralled nearly a million visitors who saw her, and taught us a lot about white shark biology. And she grew — from 5 feet and a weight of 62 pounds to 6-feet-4 1/2 inches and 162 pounds at release. Our white shark team is back in the field this summer, hoping to bring another animal back to the aquarium.

Ocean's Edge

The Monterey Bay Aquarium produces a major direct marketing campaigns annually, focused on its conservation programs. The campaign is expected to raise revenues, promote membership, and reinforce the overall brand.

One of the direct marketing pieces is called the Ocean's Edge, which is a typical direct marketing piece. "We see direct mail as an opportunity to introduce our brand to new audiences, as well as generate revenue," says Ales. "A visit to the aquarium is a visually inspiring experience, and we strive to emulate that through all our fundraising efforts and touchpoints." A combination of graphic components—including large color photographs, illustrations, and headlines—are designed to communicate content to the audience simply and quickly. "Building trust and emotional connections through direct mail requires respect for the recipient's intelligence, time, and attention," Ales notes.

The Ocean's Edge package is made up of a six-panel brochure, a response form, letterhead, a carrier envelope, and a return envelope. The brochure is printed 6/6 with one press pass per side, plus in-line aqueous coating on 120 lb. coated recycled white cover stock. The carrier envelope and letterhead are printed in combination, 6/0, with one press pass on 100 percent postconsumer waste white 70 lb. text. Paper and printing are both FSC certified.

The Ocean's Edge campaign consists of 125,000 packagesat a total cost of approximately $135,000, includingpaper, printing, shipping, mail house fees, and postage. In the first six months, the campaign raised $1.65 million.

> The communications program presents one clear and consistent voice, a vital component in maintaining the aquarium's leadership position.
>
> **JIM ALES** – design director of Monterey Bay Aquarium

It's Never Easy Being Green

Even though the Seafood Watch Guides were featured in the *New York Times Magazine's* "100 Best Ideas" issue and have received press attention from major news outlets, the design team faced both internal and external opposition when they presented strategy that stressed simplicity and positive messaging. "We positioned the program to empower consumers through trust rather than guilt," Ales says. He and his team also made it a priority to avoid the typical "eco-styling" as part of their overall brand strategy. "Several organizations had introduced similar campaigns prior to ours," Ales says. "Although well-intentioned, they failed due to a lack of design input and direction. The design component was an afterthought. This assessment won over our critics and helped us get past some early hurdles regarding our design strategy."

Ales firmly believes that "green" as a category (starting with Earth Day 1970) has been too narrowly defined. As a result, he believes that designers now face an uphill battle in combating preconceived and ingrained biases. It has become a personal goal for Ales and his team to redefine how a conservation brand can be presented.

Monterey Bay Aquarium Brand Guidelines	These guidelines were established in 2005: • Introduce imagery and messaging that inspires ownership • Feature live animal photography • Enhance visual impact, using full color when appropriate • Incorporate custom proprietary logotype • Partner with vendors winning FSC and Green e certifications • Initiate and use a policy that incorporates a strict set of vendor requirements through all production channels

TRICYCLE INC.

"Tricycle is a Sustainable Design Company" reads the sign on the front door of the company's Chattanooga, Tennessee, headquarters. This phrase confuses and entices visitors and clients alike. Michael Hendrix, cofounder and chief brand officer, is often asked, "Just what does Tricycle do? Graphic design, technology design, product design, or environmental design?" Hendrix's answer is, "All of the above." He reframes the question and suggests that sustainable design can be defined broadly as a way of thinking and set of common objectives rather than specific outcomes. This is an important distinction for a company whose output ranges from books and brochures to computer simulations, exhibit spaces, and websites.

"Tricycle's creations help create sustainable products, processes, programs, education, materials, etc." Hendrix says. "Our means are varied, but there is a single goal of creating economic, environmental, and social profitability on a long-term view. We improve processes, change corporate cultures, introduce efficiencies, identify wastefulness, improve communication, and create wealth. We do it by integrating into established manufacturing processes, marketing mechanisms, and purchasing cycles; deep dives are what produce change, otherwise it's just more treading water."

Tricycle's headquarters in
Chattanooga, Tennessee

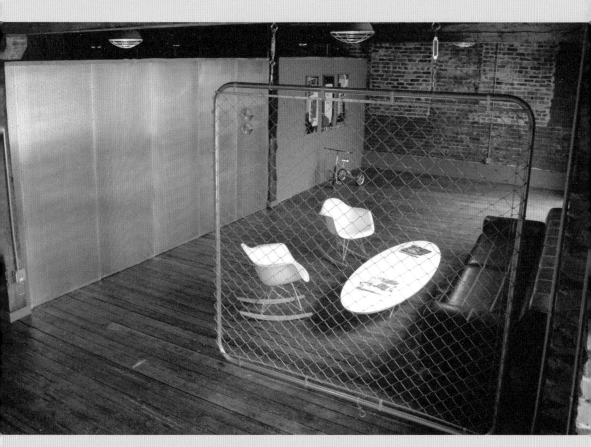

NeoCon trade show exhibit
promoting SIM from Tricycle

In a two-year period, users of our programs conserved more than 25,000 gallons of oil and kept more than 150,000 pounds of carpet samples out of American landfills, as well as creating a positive economic impact of more than $19 million.

JONATHAN BRAGDON – cofounder and president of Tricycle

Tricycle was launched in 2002 with the goal of transforming the interiors industry using designers, engineers, and business managers who believed that there were opportunities to improve efficiency and reduce waste in an industry with a large presence in the Southeastern United States. In the past six years, Tricycle has brought new life to the well-worn phrase, "Think globally, act locally." "Tricycle's founders came together around similar goals, on two different continents," said cofounder and president Jonathan Bragdon. "Today from our offices in Chattanooga and Leeds, England, we are bettering economic, social, and environmental profitability for an industry as a whole."

"One of my primary reasons for cofounding Tricycle was the search for a career with greater meaning and social significance," Hendrix adds. After several years as a practicing designer, he was ready for a change. "I began to believe it was possible to change the way design works, to benefit the designer, client, and larger society."

Tricycle's work is based on several core services. SIM from Tricycle uses computer simulations of carpet to create a sustainable sampling system that is a fast and accurate way for interior design professionals to narrow pattern and color options before requesting physical samples for final decisions. Tricycle's Environmental Calculator helps manufacturers and design professionals predict their environmental impact by using simulated samples in early rounds of product specification. Paired with a full line of design services—including trade show design, publication design, branding, and Web design—Tricycle's simulation and calculation services enable consumers to make better decisions for the environment and track their progress as they do so. Tricycle's goal is not to rid the interiors industry of carpet. Instead, Tricycle helps businesses and manufacturers become more efficient, minimize waste, and increase awareness of sustainable issues.

Erase Waste

Tricycle had developed carpet simulation tools, but there was still the challenge of getting industry professionals and manufacturers to adopt their services. Initially mills were interested in these measures purely for the cost savings. Rather than attacking the manufacturers, Tricycle decided to appeal directly to design professionals—emphasizing that they could take a proactive role in minimizing the waste generated by their industry. The resulting media campaign included an online savings calculator, an informational tradeshow booth for NeoCon (2005), trade publication advertising, and a viral sticker campaign.

Hendrix describes sampling as a problem of excess: Manufacturers push samples into the marketplace, and designers expect to receive these samples. "We set out to highlight the environmental impact of the process and encouraged both parties to become accountable for the transaction," Hendrix says. "We then provided a viable solution to reducing the waste without reducing choices."

As part of the Erase Waste campaign, Tricycle gave away stickers in tins. They asked designers to place the stickers on the back of regular carpet samples and return them to the manufacturers. "This was a risky move and, in fact, we received a very angry call from one company president," Hendrix says. "But three months later, she made a public apology to us. She had converted!"

Customers embraced the effective campaign, and carpet mills began using Tricycle data and messaging in their own marketing. The overall mission of all of Tricycle's products and services is to increase efficiency, minimize waste, and contribute to a more sustainable industry. These overarching goals are more important in the long run than specing recycled paper.

*Erase Waste stickers were given out in tins and used by interiors
professionals to send unwanted sample books back to manufacturers.*

Print advertisements gave facts about how much waste was generated by each carpet sample. These ads ran in trade publications and were targeted at industry professionals who Tricycle believed would be sympathetic to the cause.

In addition to print ads and the viral sticker campaign, Tricycle introduced its services and sought to educate manufacturers and consumers at NeoCon 2005. "In general we try to use easily recyclable materials or reusable materials for our exhibitions," says Michael Hendrix. Here, he lists the following steps taken for Tricycle's tradeshow booth designs.

LAMPS NOW ILLUMINATE THE COMPANY KITCHEN AREA

USING SHREDDED SIMULATIONS AND DOCUMENTS FROM THE OFFICE FOR THE "POLES"

THE DUMP TRUCKS AND OIL CANS ARE REUSED FOR THE NEW BOOTH DESIGN THE NEXT YEAR

Reverb

Building on their unique position in the interiors industry, Tricycle was inspired to share stories from manufacturers, editors, and designers who had great ideas and could help to generate more sustainable conversations within the industry. The resulting book featured work and ideas of people chosen by Tricycle to encourage dialogue and promote new concepts.

"Reverb is an anthology of the moment," said Tricycle communications director and book editor Caleb Ludwick. "We asked ten writers to share their thoughts on where the interiors industry stands on sustainability in 2006, and where we should be going. The initial brief, which was no more and no less than 'Design as change agent,' produced a wonderful mixed bag of conceptual arguments, open letters, and practical 'how to's' from leading voices in the field."

Hendrix designed Reverb to be both a book and an experiment in form. Cut to three sizes—including a textbook, a flipbook, and full-size integrated design—Reverb's graphics and layouts respond to the individual content of each piece of writing, and reflect Tricycle's sensibility toward contemporary culture and a sophisticated visual aesthetic.

All of the articles featured in Reverb were donated by the authors; Tricycle donated editing and design and secured corporate sponsorship from Mohawk Fine Papers, Inc., DUSK, and Aquafil USA. The book was printed on Mohawk Options 100 percent PC, a 100 percent postconsumer waste sheet, generated with wind power, and Green Seal approved. It was printed using an FSC-certified printer. Because of the generosity of donations made by Tricycle's partner organizations, 50 percent of the sale of each book was donated to Architecture for Humanity, a nonprofit organization currently promoting architectural and design solutions to humanitarian crises in Sri Lanka, India, and on the U.S. Gulf Coast. With the assistance of exposure from design blogs and press coverage within the industry, Reverb sold out in a matter of months.

Reverb as launched at the
2006 NeoCon tradeshow

TRICYCLE

Blink

Blink is a program that grew out of Tricycle's custom sampling services provided through the Internet. Tandus, a company which produces commercial carpet, wanted to show its running line (or inventoried) products with Tricycle designed simulation services. As an integrated web and print program, Blink allows interior designers to create their own virtual custom samples for viewing online or for quick delivery of realistic print samples and room scenes. "The program allows designers to reduce the physical number of samples ordered and to avoid the unnecessary use of oil, energy, and water as well as unnecessary landfill waste," Hendrix explains.

For the design of the Tandus sample book, Tricycle designers were inspired by the paper industry promos. They eventually arrived at the idea of using pads, much like sticky notes to show product. The pads were useful in this form, plus they would also serve as a symbolic and quick reminder of the product. Though Tricycle looked at multiple formats, they ended up choosing a solution that preserved the typical sample book as closely as possible in order to maintain the expected experience. "We believe that if we can recreate experiences but change the means of having them, a person will adopt a new technology," Hendrix says.

The Tandus sample book retained an appearance that would be familiar to designers used to working with old-fashioned sampling. However, it used printed swatches to promote individual carpet samples and encouraged designers to order only physical carpet samples for final decisions.

The Blink website allows designers to preview products with online simulations and to customize specific samples to be viewed digitally or printed. The built-in room simulation service shows products in a realistic context.

Nood FloorCovering

After Bo Barber, the founder of Nood FloorCovering, which produces commercial carpet, met Tricycle employees at a tradeshow, he became interested in dematerializing Nood FloorCovering's sampling process. "Barber liked what we were doing with other mills and decided he wanted his business to be based on our technology and services," Hendrix says. With the exception of actually creating carpet designs, Tricycle was asked to position the entire Nood FloorCovering brand from the ground up, including creating the messaging and designing user experiences and sampling programs.

Nood FloorCovering adopted the policy to exclusively use eco-best practices for its entire business, instead of adopting them only for selected products or programs. As a result, sales reps began using SIM on iPods to display product samples, and Nood FloorCovering decided against giving out traditional sample folders, choosing instead to provide a sticker and a few SIMs in what they termed the "Parasitic Binder." Interior designers were encouraged to find old three-ring binders, slap Nood FloorCovering stickers on the outside, and add specs and warranty sheets only for products that they were interested in.

A repurposed Nood binder, among more standard carpet company promo pieces

THE [RE]USED SAMPLE BOOK STARTER KIT.

The [Re]Used Sample Book Starter Kit.

Directions on how to make a [Re]used sample Book

Nood FloorCovering's new brand presence, including all of the services and deliverables designed by Tricycle, were unveiled at NeoCon, where the company was immediately able to save on materials. For a previous NeoCon display, Nood FloorCovering tufted a mere 700 yards of carpet for the four products they wanted to show. Because of the simulations by Tricycle, they were able to introduce another twenty-five products without any physical tufting. Tricycle's work both with simulations and branding significantly reduced Nood FloorCovering's use of materials in the sales and sampling processes, proving that a company can remain economically viable while adopting better environmental practices.

For a small company that began by taking on a multibillion-dollar industry, Tricycle has come a long way. They have been the recipient of numerous awards for their innovative ideas and accomplished designs. Tricycle is in the enviable position of advocate and industry leader, and their work is as much about consulting and helping clients rethink their manufacturing and distribution processes as it is about the traditional visual styling that's most often associated with design.

Founders Michael Hendrix and Jonathan Bragdon are now fixtures on the lecture circuit and frequent jurors for major design awards. "Tricycle has been focused on sustainability for five years, and we sounded like aliens to most people when we started," says Hendrix. "Today we sound very trendy. Someday the trend will pass, but we will still be doing the same thing."

Tricycle's design of the Nood FloorCovering tradeshow booth at NeoCon used fewer materials and was the launch of the company's new brand identity and adoption of SIM from Tricycle.

ANOTHER LIMITED REBELLION

Another Limited Rebellion (ALR), based in Richmond, Virginia, is a socially-conscious design firm dedicated to creating high-quality communications in a sustainable manner. Principal and founder Noah Scalin didn't decide to become a graphic designer to save the world. But he wanted to make sure that the work he was doing didn't conflict with his personal ideology.

Scalin began his business by asking a two-part question that he still uses to challenge himself: "Can someone make a living doing what they enjoy and affect positive change in the world? Can I create graphic design that upholds my deepest beliefs yet still be able to feed myself?"

After a decade working for clients that range from nonprofit organizations already committed to sustainable practice, to small businesses that are pleased to have a designer take the lead on both cost savings and eco-friendly production, Scalin has proved that he is able to achieve his goals and run a successful design practice.

Can someone make a living doing what they enjoy and affect positive change in the world? Can I create graphic design that upholds my deepest beliefs yet still be able to feed myself?

NOAH SCALIN - principal and founder of Another Limited Rebellion

A Secret Sustainable Goal

When ALR takes on a project, they balance the goals of the client against the environmental impact of the piece and its production. But for Scalin, an extra incentive drives him to create lasting designs. His first goal is to make work that fully communicates his client's message. But his second and equally important goal is to create artifacts that will appeal to the viewer and inspire them to keep them as collectables, thereby prolonging the life of the materials.

ALR's overall philosophy adheres to the following principles:

- Provide high-quality design for clients whose work benefits the communities in which they are located.

- Work with clients who are not involved in the creation of cigarettes, alcohol, or weapons.

- Work with companies who are not involved in a labor dispute nor are targets of a boycott for its labor or environmental practices.

- Attempt to make designs that create a minimum of waste and do as little harm to the environment as possible.

- Encourage clients to use environmentally sensitive printing processes and materials whenever applicable to a design.

- Create pro-bono designs when possible for nonprofit organizations with extremely limited resources.

- Donate 10 percent of profits to nonprofit organizations.

Turning Two Projects into One

ALR's double-use posters/brochures for Target Margin Theater and New Georges Theater, both in New York City, are collected and saved by theater patrons and area residents. Scalin's knowledge of printing and paper choices allows him to help his clients choose the most environmentally-responsible production methods for their jobs, including recycled or FSC-certified paper and eco-friendly printers.

Efficient use of resources is never an afterthought at ALR. Instead, it is part of every design brief whether a client dictates it or not. For New Georges and Target Margin Theaters, Scalin creates two deliverables from the same sheet of paper. On one side there is a memorable poster, printed in two colors. The second side, when folded, is a one-color brochure/mailer. The client saves money and resources by printing all the materials for a season or a show in a single print run and on one sheet of paper.

Target Margin Theater promotional materials use both sides of the sheet, one color, and small presses. Forgoing any bleeds means that there is no paper wasted by trimming edges. The poster/brochures were printed using Cascades' Evolution series, which is now sold as Cascades Rolland Inspiration Ecofibre. Glacier is used for the 2004/2005 piece designed to look like a newspaper, and the Eternal Feminine 2005/2006 season is printed on Foam. Both sheets are 100 percent postconsumer waste, processed chlorine free, and printed with soy-based inks.

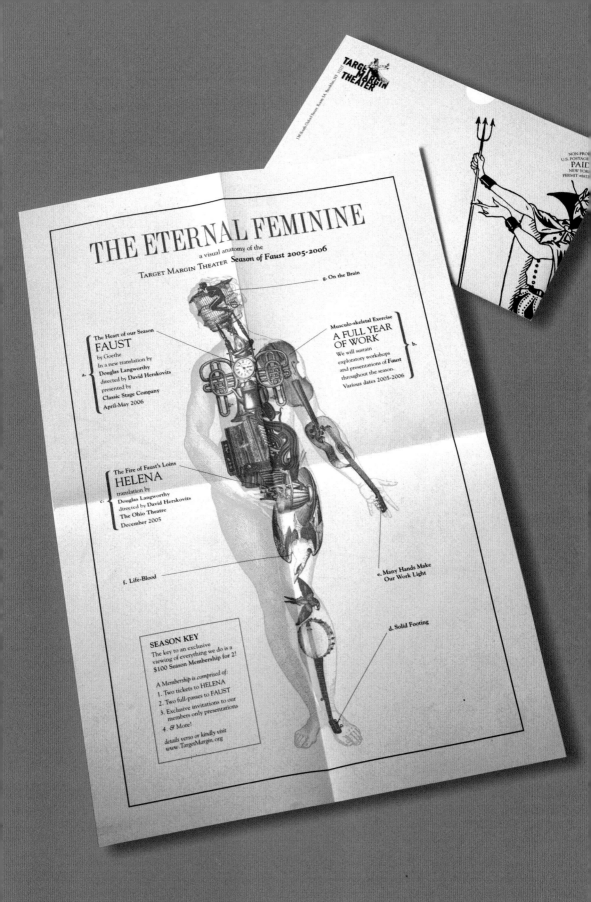

THE ETERNAL FEMININE

a visual anatomy of the

TARGET MARGIN THEATER Season of Faust 2005-2006

g. On the Brain

The Heart of our Season

FAUST

by Goethe
In a new translation by
Douglas Langworthy
directed by David Herskovits
presented by
Classic Stage Company
April-May 2006

a.

Musculo-skeletal Exercise

A FULL YEAR OF WORK

We will sustain
exploratory workshops
and presentations of *Faust*
throughout the season.
Various dates 2005-2006

b.

The Fire of Faust's Loins

HELENA

translation by
Douglas Langworthy
directed by David Herskovits
The Ohio Theatre
December 2005

c.

f. Life-Blood

e. Many Hands Make Our Work Light

d. Solid Footing

SEASON KEY

The key to an exclusive
viewing of everything we do is a
$100 Season Membership for 2!

A Membership is comprised of:
1. Two tickets to HELENA
2. Two full-passes to FAUST
3. Exclusive invitations to our
   members only presentations
4. & More!

details verso or kindly visit
www.TargetMargin.org

TARGET MARGIN THEATER

NON-PROFIT
U.S. POSTAGE
PAID
NEW YORK
PERMIT #8872

The programs for New Georges Theater use two colors and standard-size sheets. Each piece is used at least twice by the client: First for preshow promotions and later for the performance program. All materials are printed on Cascades Rolland Enviro 100, which is 100 percent postconsumer waste, processed chlorine free, FSC certified, and produced using BioGas.

Sustainable Production

When Scalin takes a job into production, he maintains the attitude that nothing is set in stone. If a printer suggests slightly resizing a project to better use a sheet or gives the option of using colors still on press from a previous job, Scalin will weigh the cost and environmental savings against his communication goals. If the alterations don't detract from the message of the piece, he willingly revises his designs. Scalin maintains that small changes can make a big difference and suggests using standard sheet sizes when possible. He reminds designers and clients alike that standards exist for a reason and that predetermined page sizes are often more cost effective and less wasteful than custom options.

Scalin has found that trying to be too perfect can be counterproductive and when people get overwhelmed by rules they often give up. To the designer who is just getting started, Scalin suggests starting small and finding a network of like-minded people. His favorites include the Graphic Alliance (www.graphicalliance.org), Social Design Notes (www.backspace.com/notes), and of course ALR's blog (www.alrdesign.com/blog).

In his own work, Scalin has found that researching one aspect of production for a job can translate into an opportunity when talking to the next client. He also uses and recommends environmental print brokers to get the best deals in environmentally responsible printing. (See "Environmental Print Brokers" on page 92.)

Environmentally Responsible Print Broker	Greg Barber isn't a printer himself; instead, he can take the specs for a job or help designers decide what environmental targets they would like to set for the printer. Barber talks to and gets quotes from a number of printers. He finds the best option for price and appropriate level of environmental compliance. The advantage of using Barber is that he deals in this area every day and can easily compare one printer's approach with another. (To read more about print brokers, see page 92.)

by Wendy E. Brawer, founding
director, Green Map System

PHOTO CREDIT: **BETH FERGUSON**

GREEN MAP SYSTEM

Green Map System (GMS), a nonprofit organization that promotes sustainable community development, based in New York City, advocates for inclusive participation in sustainable community development around the world, using mapmaking as our medium. GMS supports local Green Mapmakers as they create perspective-changing community "portraits" that act as comprehensive inventories for decision-making and as practical guides for residents and tourists. Mapmaking teams pair GMS's adaptable tools and universal iconography with local knowledge and leadership to chart green living and ecological, social, and cultural resources.

More than 300 vibrant Green Maps have been published to date, and hundreds more have been created in classrooms and workshops by kids and adults. Both the mapmaking process and the resulting Green Maps have tangible effects that accomplish the following goals:

• Strengthen local–global sustainability networks
• Expand the demand for healthier, greener choices
• Help successful initiatives spread to even more communities

Green Map System's identity is the anchor of the organization's brand and visually illustrates the organization's commitment to energizing communities worldwide to chart a sustainable future.

Maps created by GMS's partners are highly individualistic and focus on local needs and aesthetic. GMS provides tools, and a global network; mapmakers from fifty countries around the world do the rest.

Redesign of the Green Map Website and Promotion Materials

All of Green Map System's 400+ locally-led Green Map projects are unique in their perspective, and while they use the same set of icons to highlight green living, natural, social, and cultural resources, each map has its own look and feel. Helping the public navigate through and gain access to the more than 300 published Green Maps that are part of a family will raise awareness of the breadth and purpose of this movement, and provide an opportunity to review profiles of the local organizations behind individual projects as well.

For several years, GMS has distributed many of its resources in digital formats and PDFs, including the Green Map Atlas, which has already been downloaded more than 200,000 times. But, in 2006, a grant from Sappi Ideas That Matter provided funding to produce an organizational booklet and identity packet—the first in the organization's twelve year history. Designed by Millie Tien-Hui Lin, efforts to reduce the amount of paper used resulted in a small format booklet that folds into packet containing a DVD, newsletter, space for a Green Map, icon poster, press release, and financial information, as needed.

All of the deliverables in Green Map's identity system were produced with help from Sappi's Ideas. That Matter program/ competition to enter the competition, a designer creates the proposal as a pro bono contribution, and Sappi funding covers the printing and related costs of a nonprofit organization's identity campaign.

Green Map System's media kit represents efficient use of resources and smart design. Pieces from the kit can be used separately for a variety of purposes, and the full kit is striking yet small enough to be mailed easily and without a lot of extra cost for postage.

GREEN MAP

DIRECTIONS TO A SUSTAINABLE FUTURE

Energizing communities worldwide to chart a sustainable future — together! Collaboratively developed since 1995, Green Map System has empowered a diverse global movement of local mapmaking teams charting natural, social and cultural resources in their own hometowns. With award-winning global icons, multi-lingual resources, websites, workshops and regional hubs, we strengthen local sustainability networks in hundreds of cities, villages and neighborhoods. In over 50 countries, our maps bring people together to discover, share and care for their communities. Join us and explore Green Map's perspective — changing views on the world.

Think Global, Map Local!

NES
NYC EDITION

L, MAP LOCAL!

THINK GLO

For the identity packet, GMS selected Sappi's FSC-certified Opus paper. Recycled Environmental Writing paper was used for the stationery. By minimizing the use of bleed images and extensive coverage areas, the wastefulness of excessive ink coverage was addressed. The result was a clean, balanced design. A local printer with an in-house bindery was chosen to minimize the environmental impacts of shipping. The informational DVD fits into slots without the need for additional packaging, and the whole brochure can be sealed and sent with small stickers because the packet's contact information is placed as a self-mailer.

To further minimize waste when a hardcopy isn't needed, the booklet is available at www.greenmap.org as a PDF, too. It's one of hundreds of downloadable digital resources now available on the redesigned Green Map website. The website was relaunched in May 2007, in response to the need for greater public and press access to the goals, methods, and outcomes behind each map. It includes the "Greenhouse," which is a dynamic resource for and about Green Mapmaking, filled with authentic voices sharing stories from each locally-led Green Map project. Behind the scenes is the Mapmakers' Tool Center, which obviates the need to burn and mail disks, and social networking/collaboration/exchange tools to strengthen the mapmakers' collective impact. Promoting participation in sustainability at the community level is the website's purpose, and it inspires action and shares models for green living around the world.

GMS touches many communities in many nations, and having greater recognition of a global brand is a benefit to all. It establishes credibility and encourages Green Mapmakers to go further and aim higher as they research, design, and disseminate their maps. Alongside the printed resources in our identity program, a new digital style guide was created for printed Green Maps and is expected to help many achieve an excellent outcome. For our network, our supporters and our communities, reaching and motivating more participation in sustainable living is the overall goal, underscored by the brand's importance.

Green Map System's website was totally redesigned to be a portal of tools, information, and networking for mapmakers and to share their work to the public. In addition to employing a visual aesthetic in line with the organization's brand, www.greenmap.org has a sophisticated user interface that allows users to browse the public sections of the site or delve into richer content in the "member's only" section.

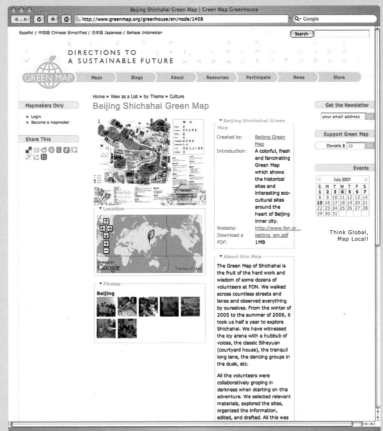

by Sarah Haun, director of marketing
and communications, Two Twelve

PHOTO BY GREG KINCH

TWO TWELVE

Like the larger environmental movement, Two Twelve's expertise in green design has
evolved over time with the help of different experiences. The firm's principals and staff have
gradually discovered and integrated sustainable principles in their personal lives, the day-
to-day workings of the office, and in the design and production of professional projects. It
didn't happen overnight, and we're not there yet. It's an ongoing process, a way of thinking,
working, and living that we eventually expect to be as natural and important as breathing.

In the realm of professional practice, Two Twelve's first serious encounter with sustainable
design came in 2003, when we prepared a proposal for a conservation organization. In con-
sidering the opportunity to redesign signage for a waterfront park, both Two Twelve and the
client recognized that while the existing sign program was ineffective, discarding it entirely
would be a waste of energy, materials, and money that would be counter to the organization's mission and budget. Two Twelve built a re-use strategy into a design proposal for the
first time in the history of the company.

While Two Twelve didn't win this particular project, the event stimulated internal dialogue
about green issues, and the organization, Scenic Hudson Land Trust, became a client for a
larger park signage system a few years later. More significantly, internal dialogue coincided
with the germ of the Green Team, a group of Two Twelve employees who made it their mission to educate the rest of the office about the issues and opportunities of sustainability in
the design business.

The original Two Twelve Green Team included staff designers Pamela Paul from the environmental graphic design practice, and Jenn Richey from the branding and print group.
Paul and Richey introduced their ideas and a framework for thinking about sustainability at
a few Lunch Labs, the company's monthly informal staff enrichment meetings. The ideas hit
home with many people in the office, and the program took off.

As is typically the case in small companies, important support came from the top, with principals Ann Harakawa and David Gibson both solidly behind the effort. Harakawa and Gibson were willing to commit time and resources, but they also expected accountability.

Harakawa grew up in Hawaii with an "islander" mentality. "When I was a kid, all you had came from the limited land around you or off a boat," she explains. "You learned to take nothing for granted." Her personal commitment to this initiative is apparent in her decision to replace the family minivan with a hybrid vehicle.

Gibson hails from Canada, and his formative years in a social democracy have shaped many aspects of the civic-minded firm he cofounded in 1980. "Taking care of the environment is another way of serving the public good," he reflects. Since Two Twelve's "greening," he and his partner have planted an organic garden at their upstate farm.

Sarah Haun, director of marketing and communications, has actively supported the Green Team by integrating sustainability in the firm's marketing materials, project proposals, and internal communications, and she encourages the marketing staff to participate in the team.

Mission Statement

Haun worked with the Green Team on one of its first initiatives: the development of an Environmental Mission Statement. This conceptual exercise clarified the team's mandate and gave it public expression. The mission was posted on the company's website and inspired the firm's annual promotional greeting for Two Twelve Day—February 12—in 2005.

This promotion highlighted Two Twelve's first consciously green production decision: the specification of Mohawk Options recycled paper stock for a major client project. "4,280 copies were made of New York City's 600-page Candidature File for the 2012 Olympic Games," read the Two Twelve Day promo. "All 2,568,000 pages were printed on paper made of 100 percent postconsumer fiber and manufactured at the first large scale paper manufacturing facility in the United States to use nonpolluting wind energy."

In addition to influencing the firm's marketing messages and print specifying practices, the Green Team began to change practical aspects of office operations. First steps were small and incremental: replacing plastic disposable pencils with more durable ones that could be refilled and collecting used batteries for proper disposal. These little changes involved everyone in the office and helped build important momentum and support for the Green Team.

After making the switch to environmentally preferable office products, Two Twelve's Green Team created labels to educate fellow employees and help them understand why the new products represent better purchasing options.

©2007 ERIK MURILLO/TWO TWELVE

This 600-page New York City candidature file for the 2012 Olympic Games was designed by Two Twelve.
©2005 TED MORRISON

Signage for Northern Arizona University's 738-acre campus

The signage system designed by Two Twelve is designed to be extendable.

©2007 JERRY FOREMAN

NAU Signage

While initially it may require more leg work and research than print design, environmental graphic design (EGD) provides many opportunities to use sustainable materials in situations that demand that design solutions have a much longer lifespan than is typical for paper products. For the Northern Arizona University (NAU) campus in Flagstaff, Two Twelve designed a signage system that responded to the harsh desert mountain climate and created sustainable yet highly durable solutions. Working closely with landscape architects EDAW, Two Twelve conducted a thorough wayfinding analysis to determine appropriate areas for pathways and landscaping throughout the campus. To keep the program's environmental impact to a minimum, signs were constructed using a variety of sustainable materials including natural sandstone from a local quarry, durable porcelain (eliminating the need for frequent repairs and replacements), recyclable acrylic, and mechanical hardware instead of adhesives wherever possible.

Two Twelve continues to seek projects that can incorporate green principles and practices, and it also targets prospective client organizations, such as mass transit agencies, that support sustainable living in the public realm. This has allowed Two Twelve to expand their client base and increase the scope of projects that the company takes on. One of the firm's key projects in this area has been the design of materials supporting PlaNYC, Mayor Bloomberg's 2007 initiative to prepare New York for the addition of one million new residents by 2030, while also contributing to the fight against global climate change. Staff designer Michelle Cates, who managed the PlaNYC projects says, "As a designer, it's incredibly exciting to be informed and prepared to address sustainable issues with clients."

In 2005, Two Twelve got involved in "GROW," the AIGA New York Chapter's (AIGA-NY) first full-day conference dedicated to the intersection of design, sustainability, and business in New York City. Haun served on the event committee with Marc Alt, a fellow AIGA-NY board member at the time, and the chair of the conference. Two Twelve designed a promotion piece for the event.

Two Twelve's print designers, including Michelle Cates and Whitney Grant, worked with Alt and Don Carli, senior research fellow at the Institute for Sustainable Communication, to produce a poster printed on recycled paper with richly layered information to provoke designers to "Start a Discussion" about sustainable design.

"In the end, it was a more complex project than we anticipated," says Haun. "But the investment of time and thought in green issues helped raise awareness within the office and, we hope, the larger design community. It made it patently clear to us that sustainability is not about easy answers."

RESOURCES

Sustainability is a moving target. The constant evolution in materials and processes makes keeping up with best practices a dizzying task. In the past several years designers, professional organizations, and nongovernmental organizations have created a range of great online resources that designers can take advantage of. These sites often offer the most up-to-date (and location specific) information on environmentally responsible printers, new paper products, and trends in sustainable communications design. Many also include networking, paper guides, and vendor checklists.

AIGA Center for Sustainable Design

Through case studies, interviews, resources, and discourse, this site provides information to graphic designers who want to incorporate sustainable thinking into their professional lives. www.sustainability.aiga.org

Conservatree

This site seeks to be a one-stop source for information on environmental papers. It includes information about the environmental ramifications of the paper industry and advice for both large and small-scale purchasers. www.conservatree.com

Design Can Change

This Canadian resource and networking site helps designers who want to work together to combat climate change. www.designcanchange.org

Design By Nature

This Australian site offers general information on sustainability for graphic designers including info on paper, forestry, printing, a sample print spec sheet, as well as a case studies section on the work of environmentally-conscious Australian designers. Design By Nature has some of the most extensive information on eco-friendly printing available. www.designbynature.org

RESOURCES

Environmental Paper Network

This site is graphic design specific, but it offers a lot of information about environmentally preferable paper options, and it is hosted by environmental organizations. www.environmentalpaper.org

GreenBlue

Founded by *Cradle to Cradle* authors William McDonough and Michael Braungart, GreenBlue is now an autonomous nonprofit institute that helps professional communities create practical solutions, resources, and opportunities for implementing sustainability. They are a great resource if you are dealing with packaging or work for a large corporation that can afford to join their corporate partnerships. Also see Sustainable Packaging Coalition, which is an industry working group spinoff of GreenBlue. www.greenblue.org, www.sustainablepackaging.org

Institute for Sustainable Communications (ISC)

ISC helps advocate for and connect professionals and companies in the communications sector with tools that promote economic, social, and environmentally-sound business practices. The Responsible Enterprise Print (REP) program, developed by the ISC, identifies opportunities for organizations to reduce costs, reduce environmental impacts, improve organizational effectiveness, and enhance stakeholder relationships. www.sustaincom.org

Japan for Sustainability

This website, which is available in both English and Japanese, is not graphic design specific, but it is run by a dedicated group of people who are very good about putting interested parties in touch with each other and giving general information about sustainability in Japan. www.japanfs.org

Lovely as a Tree

Based in England, this website seeks to provides the answers to what a graphic designer needs to know to be more environmentally aware. It provides a great interactive printfinder feature that lets users choose by type of service as well as location. www.lovelyasatree.com

MetaFore

The organization's Environmental Paper Assessment Tool provides consistent language and metrics for buyers and sellers of paper products to discuss the environmental ramifications of purchasing decisions. Note: MetaFore primarily works with large brand-name businesses. www.metafore.org

O2 Global Network

This international global network for sustainable issues is a great resource if you are looking to network with people working sustainably in your area or need information but live in an out-of-the way place. With new chapters popping up regularly, you can find people who are willing to talk, educate, and share resources all over the world. www.o2.org

Organic Design Operatives (ODO)

This is a diverse collective of creative people who are brought together by the common mission of connecting people with nature by design. The site offers an eco-design tool kit, print spec worksheet, a networking feature, and a section on case studies. www.themightyodo.com

Papierpraat (Dutch only)

This site provides information to make printers and designers aware of everything that has to do with paper and its use and recycling. The links page is an extensive list of resources, with descriptions of their use or services, both in the Netherlands and beyond. www.papierpraat.nl

Re-nourish

A U.S.-based informational and networking site put together by Eric Benson, the site includes lists of green paper and printers; info on printing, paper, and packaging; and a case studies section. Re-nourish has its own blog, reprints articles, and offers lots of links to topics of interest. www.re-nourish.com

Sustainable Design Online

This Minneapolis College of Art and Design certificate program was created for working professionals to improve their knowledge of sustainable practice, theory, and techniques. It may be the best way for designers to learn about sustainability in a guided setting. Students can enroll a single course or take the full eighteen-credit certificate program. www.mcad.edu (Look under "Continuing Studies.")

Treehugger

Probably the most well-known site for information on green solutions, products, and news. The site has area-specific blogs that are updated daily. Treehuggeer is often one of the first media outlets to break news on sustainable issues. www.treehugger.com

Waterless Printing Association (WPA)

This organization provides information about cost, speed, color, and environmental benefits of waterless printing. The organization's website makes general information available to the public, lists printers offering waterless lithography, and provides experts who can explain the benefits of switching to this system. Additional information and services are available to the WPA's member organizations. www.waterless.org

GLOSSARY

Agricultural fibers: Fiber harvested from tree-free organic sources that are grown specifically for use in paper production, also called "tree-free."

Agricultural residues: Fibers recovered from annual crops usually planted as food crops or for commercial use (corn, sugar cane, and wheat) that is used to make paper. The use of these fibers is usually limited to areas where crops are grown locally.

Carbon dioxide: A heavy colorless, odorless gas that results from the combustion of carbon found in organic materials. It's the gas most closely associated with global climate change.

Chlorine: A chemical used in the bleaching process to give paper its white appearance and to remove lignin, which is a naturally occurring material that can yellow over time (as in newsprint).

De-inking: The process of removing ink and other contaminates from collected paper. De-inking is usually done at a separate facility and finished fiber is sent to paper manufacturers.

Dioxins: Refers to a group of toxic substances that are produced during the paper production processes when pulp is exposed to elemental chlorine. The effects of dioxins on the environment and human health are not fully understood but have been associated with cancer and birth defects.

Effluent: Waste in liquid (most often water) that is discharged from a mill, or other manufacturing facility and can end up in the ground water.

Elemental chlorine-free (ECF): A label that indicates fibers have been bleached without elemental chlorine and is instead made with chlorine derivatives such as chlorine dioxide ($ClO2$).

Forest Stewardship Council (FSC): An independent third party certifier of sustainably harvested virgin fiber and mixed use recycled content. In order to use the FSC logo as an environmental claim on paper, the product must have flowed through the FSC "chain-of-custody" from the FSC-certified forest, to a paper manufacturer, merchant, and finally printer who have FSC chain-of-custody certification.

Intact forests: See "old growth."

Mill broke: Paper waste generated by the mill that can be reused in the manufacturing process. Mill broke may make up a fairly large percentage of recycled content so it is preferable to ask what percentage of the content is derived from postconsumer waste and where the rest comes from. (See "preconsumer waste.")

Old growth: Also called "intact forests" (included in this category are boreal and rainforest). Natural forests that have been allowed to grow naturally over a long period of time (in excess of 100 years) and have developed into complete ecosystems containing every stage of tree life as well as the appropriate bio-diversity of other plants and animals.

Preconsumer waste: Refers to materials that include trip or scrap from the manufacturing process and printers, or even over-runs that are reused to make new products.

Postconsumer waste: End product that has reached the consumer used and then collected to make new material rather than end up in a landfill or incinerator.

Process chlorine-free (PCF): A label used to refer to recycled fiber that was not bleached using chlorine or chlorine derivatives but that may have been bleached using chlorine during the paper's initial production and therefore may not be totally chlorine-free.

Recycled paper: Paper coming from either post- or preconsumer waste. Recycled pulp can be made into the same variety and quality of paper stock that is made from virgin fiber.

Totally chlorine-free (TCF): A label that indicates fiber has been produced without the use of chlorine in the bleaching process or is unbleached.

TCF and PCF both use benign elements such as oxygen, ozone, or hydrogen peroxide for the bleaching process. Most scientists and environmentalist, believe that Totally Chlorine Free production is preferable to Elemental Chlorine Free bleaching.

Tree-free: Includes paper products made from agricultural residues, nontree fibers, and more recently, products made from minerals and plastics. Please note: Tree-free does not necessarily denote more environmentally preferable products.

Triple-bottom line: (People, Planet, and Profit) refers to a balanced exchange of goods and services (beyond just profit) that takes into account the economic, environmental, and social implications of an organizations' output and performance.

Volatile organic compounds (VOCs): Refers to a broad class of organic gasses that includes vapors from solvents, inks, and gasoline. Minimizing or eliminating the use of products that produce VOCs is important because these compounds can react with other materials to form ozone, the major ingredient of smog.

Virgin fiber: Refers to paper pulp fiber that is derived directly from its organic source.

ENDNOTES

Chapter 1: *Overview of Sustainable Design*

1. Benyus, Janine. 2002. *Biomimicry: Innovation Inspired by Nature*. New York: Harper Perennial. Paraphrased from preface.

2. Benyus, Janine. 2002. *Biomimicry: Innovation Inspired by Nature*. New York: Harper Perennial p.7.

3. Paraphrased from A Conversation with Janine Benyus at http://64.233.167.104/ search?q=cache:mlKERn_Nad4J:www.biomimicry.net/conversationwithjanineA.htm+bio mimicry+will+it+last+will+it+fit&hl=en&ct=clnk&cd=1&gl=us

4. William McDonaugh and Michael Braungart. 2002. *Cradle to Cradle*. New York: North Point Press, p. 90, 91.

5. Strategies paraphrased from expanded text describing these strategies on pages 10 and 11 of *Natural Capitalism*.

Chapter 3: *The Science and Practice of Sustainable Design Forestry*

1. Paper Task Force report, p. 170. A free copy of this report is available for download at: http://www.environmentaldefense.org/article.cfm?contentid=1689.

2. Allen Hershkowitz, Bronx Ecology, 2002, p. 75.

3. "Toward a Sustainable Paper Cycle: An Independent Study on the Sustainability of the Pulp and Paper Industry," 1996, commissioned by the International Institute for Environment and Development for the World Business Council For Sustainable Development.

4. United Nations Environment Programme (UNEP), www.unep.org.

5. Website of the Rainforst Alliance, www.rainforest-alliance.org.

6. Website for Forest Stewardship Council, www.fsc.org/en/about.

7. Paper Task Force Report, p. 170.

8. Paper Task Force Report, p. 172.

9. See the *Design by Nature Guide to Printing and the Environment* at www.designbynature.org.

10. Website of Xerox Corporation, www.xerox.com/go/xrx/template/009. jsp?view=Feature&ed_name=CSR_Feature_iGen3&Xcntry=USA&Xlang=en_US.

DESIGNER INDEX

Another Limited Rebellion
2701 Edgewood Ave.
Richmond, VA 23222
USA
www.ALRdesign.com

Aurus Estudio Grafico
Rua Paulo de Deus Bessa
398 Santo Inacio
Curbita, Parana 82300-210
Brazil
www.aurus.art.br

Blake Coglianese
University of North Florida
Art & Design
1 UNF Drive
Jacksonville, FL 32224
USA
Email: bcoglian@unf.edu
www.focusednrg.com

Design Action Collective
1710 Franklin St. #300
Oakland, CA 94612
USA
www.designaction.org

Design by Nature
www.designbynature.org
Egmont UK
egmont.co.uk

Green Map System
P.O. Box 249
New York, NY 10002-0244
USA
www.greenmap.org

Guerrini Design Island
Paraguay 754
4B (PC 1057)
Buenos Aires
Argentina
www.guerriniisland.com

Austin Happel
275 Union Blvd.
Apt. 209
St. Louis, MO 63
USA
www.austinhappel.com

Michael B. Hardt
27 Rue Principale
F57980 Diebling
France
www.michael-hardt.com

INDEX

Heller Communication Design
15 Broad Street No. 1712
New York, NY
USA
www.hellercd.com

Main 5 Design
35-27 80th Street
#22
Jackson Heights, NY 11372
USA
www.main5design.com

Milani Design
Via Viva 1021
20122 Milano
Italy
www.moulin3arcs.com

MIO
340 North 12th Street
Unit 301
Philadelphia, PA 19107
USA
www.mioculture.com

Monterey Bay Aquarium
886 Cannery Row
Monterey, CA 93940
USA
www.montereybayaquarium.com

NAU
1624 N.W. Lovejoy Street
Portland, OR
USA
www.nau.com

People Tree
www.peopletree.com

Plazm
PO Box 2863
Portland, OR 97208
USA
www.plazm.com

Re-nourish.com
1007 S. Victor Street
Champaign, IL 61821
USA
www.re-nourish.com

Carol Sogard
University of Utah, Department of
Art and Art History
375 South 1530 East Room 161
Salt Lake City, UT 84112
USA
Email: c.sogard@art.utah.edu

Tiger Mountain Innovations, Inc.
14221 NE 190th St.
Suite 150
Woodinville, WA 98072
USA
www.squakmountainstone.com

TRICYCLE Inc.
3001 Broad Street
STE 200
Chattanooga, TN 37409
USA
www.tricycleinc.com

Two Twelve
902 Broadway
Floor 20
New York, NY 10010
USA
www.twotwelve.com

Vegetablefriedrice.com
61 Regents Studios
8 Andrews Road
London, E84QN
UK
www.vegetablefriedrice.com

VIOLA Eco-Graphic Design
Level 4
247 Flinders Lane
Melbourne, Victoria 3000
Australia
www.violadesign.com.au

Hoseob Yoon
Kookmin University
861-1
Jeung Neung-Dong
Seungbuk-Ku, Seoul
Korea
www.greencanvas.com

ABOUT THE AUTHOR

Aaris Sherin is an educator, writer, and designer. She is currently an assistant professor of graphic design at St. John's University in Queens, New York. She holds a bachelor's of fine arts degree from the School of the Art Institute of Chicago and a master's of fine arts degree from Rochester Institute of Technology.

With research interests spanning both historical and contemporary issues, Sherin works in areas that include sustainable design practice and theory, the history of women in design, and hybrid research practices. Sherin uses original source material and journalistic methods to uncover areas of design practice that have been overlooked and/or merit greater attention. As guest editor for *GroveArt* (Oxford University Press), she supervised the addition of more than thirty entries on female designers as part of the 2006 Women in the Arts update. Sherin is a frequent lecturer and speaker at both national and international design conferences. Her writing has been featured in *PRINT*, *STEP Inside Design*, *GroveArt* (Oxford University Press), and *Leonardo* (MIT Press).